D1309956

EDUCATION FOR FREEDOM:
The Philosophy of Education
of
Jacques Maritain

Printed and Bound in Canada

The translation of this work has been subsidized by the Canada Council.

© University of Ottawa Press, 1982.
ISBN-2-7603-1157-0

LB
880
.M3332 –
A4413

EDUCATION FOR FREEDOM:
The Philosophy of Education
of
Jacques Maritain

by
JEAN-LOUIS ALLARD

Translated by Professor RALPH C. NELSON,
University of Windsor

Preface by Dr. DONALD A. GALLAGHER

UNIVERSITY OF NOTRE DAME
PRESS
Notre-Dame, Indiana

UNIVERSITY OF OTTAWA
PRESS
Ottawa, Canada

1982

Canadian Cataloguing in Publication Data

Allard, Jean-Louis, 1926-
    Education for freedom

(Education; no. 7)
Translation of: L'éducation à la liberté.
Bibliography: p.
ISBN 2-7603-1157-0

1. Maritain, Jacques, 1882-1973—Philosophy. 2. Education—Philosophy. 3. Liberty. I. Title. II.
Series: Education (University of Ottawa Press); no. 7.

LB775.M3568A4413   370'.1   C82-090083-4

Preface

In this Maritain Centenary year, Professor Allard's invitation to write a foreword or preface to his book is doubly appreciated. It provides me with an opportunity to say something about the philosophical significance of the Christian philosopher to whom I am so deeply indebted and it arouses recollections of the association I enjoyed with Jean-Louis Allard in the Faculty of Philosophy at the University of Ottawa during the 1970s. In this bilingual institution, the Faculty of Education offered a course entitled in French Philosophes-Educateurs *on outstanding educator-philosophers from classical to modern times, and which I taught in English and Dr. Allard, thoroughly at home in both languages, taught to both francophone and anglophone students. We shared, I think, a perspective in which the educational philosophers (Plato, Rousseau, Dewey and others) were viewed at one and the same time first in terms of the social environment and the cultural institutions of their times (Plato and the Athenian youth, Rousseau acting as tutor to the gentry of his day, Dewey the teacher of pedagogy and of "democratic education" in Teachers' College) and secondly in terms of their "eternal" significance as thinkers philosophising upon educating and teaching, and of their lasting contributions (however profoundly one disagrees with certain of their positions and in some cases with the very bases of their philosophy) to educational thought.*

The contribution to educational philosophy made by Jacques Maritain (and he was given a place of honor on the roster of Great Educators by Professor Allard and by myself in the course we taught) is profoundly philosophical and forthrightly Christian. A Christian philosophy of education (as he names it in the first chapter of Education at the Crossroads*) is distinctively philosophical because it fully recognizes the implications of the existence of the human being in various and diverse spheres and sets forth an educational program for the full development of the person. It is distinctively Christian because it incorporates insights which Maritain himself calls "fructifications of Christian thought", liberal education for all, the primacy of the contemplative spirit, the dignity of manual work and the conquest of freedom.*

Maritain's educational works, unlike the case of Dewey's, are not usually considered to be among his major contributions to philosophy. He himself often refers to these and other works, even some of his greatest, as "sketches" in that they are simply outlines of larger studies he hoped to complete and in that they are intended as starting points for fellow-Thomists and collaborators to join in the same task. However, the word "sketch" should not mislead us. This Christian educational philosopher has extraordinary range as well as depth. His thought ranges from the rigourous and technical treatment of specifically philosophical questions, to topics of current importance involving religious, social, pedagogical aspects, to a lofty vision that is poetic and verging on the mystical, as when in the chapter entitled "Todo y Nada" in the Degrees of Knowledge, he assails that "inverse phenomenon" of our time, the "spirituality of the flesh", "a kind of ascesis and a martyrdom of the passing moment subjugating souls". Where atheism has become the religion of the State, it exercises "a painstaking pedagogical surgery" on souls "to extirpate from them the image of God." Yet we should not flatter ourselves. "Western liberalism has stifled childhood" with "education by omission". And the endeavors of the Christian humanist tradition have all too often been lacking to the extent that they have not comprehended how fixed has become the shift to a secularistic outlook and "life-style" and to the extent that they have not responded with positive solutions and programs. In the field of education, Jacques Maritain has responded positively, as the book of Jean-Louis Allard demonstrates cogently. Insights abound in his work, and not infrequently they are uttered in a striking sentence but scarcely developed; the most significant, and one rich in implications is Maritain's insight into freedom of autonomy or expansion and into its meaning as the goal of education. Professor Allard has in his turn chosen the theme of liberty with unerring judgment as the key to Maritain's educational thought.

The "conquest of freedom" theme is taken up again and again by Maritain. The term "conquer" does not do full justice in my opinion to the depth of his thought on this topic. Rather than "warlike" victory, one should imagine the scaling of mountaintops, the ascent of the mind to the peaks of liberty. He himself spoke of the mystics who reached "the heroic peaks of human life". In his credo (Confession de foi) presented in English in the collaborative work I Believe, Jacques Maritain refers to the pursuit of liberty in the order of the spiritual life and in the social and political order. In the first, the human person "aspires to perfect and absolute freedom and therefore to a superhuman state". In the order of temporal life, it is a liberty proportionate to his human state to which man aspires; "society is intended to develop conditions of life in common which, while insuring first of all advantages and peace to the whole, help each person in a positive manner progressively to conquer this freedom of expansion."

In his works on social and political philosophy, notably in The Rights of Man and the Natural Law and Christianity and Democracy, the attainment of freedom of expansion and autonomy is presented as the political task. Every political philosophy, it is true, represents itself as pursuing this aim. But, Maritain points out, there is a conquest of freedom which is illusory and false and one which is true and fulfiling. He points out further (in The Rights of Man) that this freedom of expansion "consists above all in the flowering of moral and rational life and of those ("immanent") interior activities which are the intellectual and moral virtues".

It is in the essay "The Conquest of Freedom" that Jacques Maritain explains most fully his thought on freedom of independence (autonomy, expansion, fulfilment) and the connatural and transnatural aspirations of the person. I recall the late Dr. Joseph Evans, first Director of the Jacques Maritain Center at Notre Dame University, remarking that this study, which does not really speak of education, is at the heart of Maritain's educational theory. The remarks above indicate, and the work of Professor Allard thoroughly explores and establishes why liberty or freedom is the goal of true liberal education. Aided by his long experience in teaching, research and writing in the field of educational philosophy, he has taken this key theme, cette idée maîtresse, *and set it forth in a remarkably clear and compelling fashion; furthermore, he has developed and deepened it in the light of present day educational thought as well as of Thomistic philosophy. Maritain himself, as was said above, with his characteristic modesty, claimed to provide us merely with a sketch of a vast project remaining to be completed. He called for disciples or rather collaborators to elaborate a fully autonomous and articulated philosophical anthropology, likewise a philosophical ethics and likewise a philosophy of education. To this common task for Christian and Thomist philosophy (terms which did not altogether satisfy Maritain but which he continued to employ even in his later writings) Jean-Louis Allard has made a significant contribution destined to have lasting influence in the field of educational philosophy. It is a contribution not only to Maritain studies but to the perennial philosophical question of liberty of autonomy and expansion as the key to the understanding of the truly human formation of the person.*

Donald A. GALLAGHER, Ph. D.
President,
American Maritain Association

ACKNOWLEDGMENTS

I wish to express my gratitude to all those who have greatly encouraged me in this project of an English edition of my book *L'éducation à la liberté ou La philosophie de l'éducation de Jacques Maritain* (Les Editions de l'Université d'Ottawa, 1978). The following words from an American scholar aptly summarize the many encouragements I have received: ''Maritain's views on education are important and timely, and a translation of your book would make a valuable contribution to the literature on the topic.''

I am grateful, above all, to Professor Ralph C. Nelson who has so expertly translated my book, to Dr. Donald A. Gallagher for his thoughful and inspiring Preface, and to the Editors for willingly publishing this book.

Jean-Louis ALLARD
University of Ottawa

Preface
to the French Edition

There are several reasons why the excellent study which Jean-Louis Allard devotes to Jacques Maritain's philosophy of education merits attention. The fact is that Maritain doesn't yet occupy the place that is rightfully his in the philosophical literature of the French language and fortunately Professor Allard's work will contribute to enriching a bibliography which is all too thin. On the other hand, this work is concerned with the least known aspect of Maritain's thought. Indeed, insofar as an implicit or explicit pedagogy is essential to any philosophy, this aspect nevertheless is not to be neglected. And Personalism has played a sufficiently important role in the history of thought in our century to make us curious to know about a pedagogy which directly appeals to it. Moreover, this pedagogy answers to the concerns of our time, and by stressing freedom, it meets with one of the most important trends of contemporary educational thought, while at the same time it specifies and deepens it.

Those would be reasons enough to be pleased with the publication of Allard's work. But there is also the reason, which takes on a special prominence today, that it deals with the philosophy of education. In fact, by a strange paradox, it may be noted that few, among the many different works on pedagogical problems, strive to answer the question of the aims of education, which one would have thought so essential.

Methods are readily dealt with and the progressive school is tirelessly contrasted with the traditional school; the relations between parents and children and between teachers and pupils are anxiously examined; passionate dissertations appear on the ideological function of education and its class character; doctors and psychiatrists are consulted like oracles; investigations multiply, statistics are solicited, etc... but the very simple, if not easy, question is hardly raised — the one put by Victor Hugo:

"After all, what can the purpose of all this be?"

That scientists could reply to the poet that his question, in fact, was that of a poet, not a scientist, is true. Science is the knowledge of the world as it is and it need not worry about the problem of aims. Meteorology forecasts rain or shine without being concerned whether the earth needs water or sun. The philosopher can indeed theorize about the vocation and destiny of man; the man of science confines himself to the positive examination of the conditions of man's existence. Indeed, insofar as the disciplines which deal with education seek to be scientific, it is understandable that they are indifferent to a properly philosophical problem.

In this respect, nothing is more significant than the new national regulation in France which defines the content of the licentiate and master's degree in the educational sciences. A minimum of 350 hours of teaching is provided for each year of study and this instruction is classified under fifteen headings, two-thirds of which are required subjects, one-third optional. Now nowhere in these headings do we find the slightest inducement to reflect on the problem of the aims of education. Strictly speaking, it could only be mentioned by cleverly interpreting the adjective "interdisciplinary" under the heading "interdisciplinary studies in the operation and development of educational systems".

Thus, thanks to these new programs, future French specialists in education will know all there is to know about the means of arriving at an end, of which nothing was ever said to them. They will have analyzed "the behaviour of agents, partners, and groups in the midst of learning situations", they will have examined "modern methods and techniques of education", they will be instructed in "the methodology of the disciplines", they will be acquainted with the subtleties of "evaluation and the scientific study which tends to improve testing methods", etc..., but if they were asked why we send children to school, they will doubtless answer that it is by virtue of an old law which makes education compulsory.

Perhaps it will be said that quite obviously the aim of education is the formation of man and that subject does not warrant lengthy elaborations. But can we hide the fact today that the very definition of man is the most controversial of all topics? And are not these controversies appropriately philosophical? The question of knowing whether man is a recent invention, destined to an early end, does not derive from the sciences of education and yet it must be answered in order to state what education ought to be. It is true that this answer is usually implicit, but that is regrettable. The problem of foundations or principles in every sense of the word is essential here, and the claim to resolve it without having clearly set down the issue beforehand is annoying.

Jacques Maritain was particularly aware of the need to provide a philosophical grounding for any discourse on pedagogy and he did not conceal the fact that his reflections on education stemmed from his philosophy of freedom. By entitling his book Education for Freedom, *Jean-Louis Allard has underlined very well the intimate connection between ends and means. When he speaks of what Maritain calls "liberal education for all", he does not run the risk of falling into the misunderstandings which forced Neill to write, after his work on the free child in* Summerhill, *the subsequent work* Freedom — not license! *For if almost all contemporary pedagogies are pedagogies of freedom, few of them take the precaution of stating at the outset in what freedom consists. One of the finest features of Allard's book is that through Maritain's work, it makes us sensitive to this basic subordination of any genuine pedagogy to philosophy.*

Georges PASCAL, *Professor,*
The University of the Social Sciences
of Grenoble (France).

Table of Contents

Preface.. vii
Acknowledgments x
Preface to the French Edition.. xi
Translator's Forword xv
Abbreviations... xvi

INTRODUCTION 1
1. Jacques Maritain, Thomistic Philosopher............................ 2
2. Jacques Maritain, Christian Philosopher............................. 3
3. Maritain, Philosopher of Being 4
4. Maritain, Philosopher of Education 7

Chapter One. MARITAIN'S PERSONALISM.................................... 11
1. The Scientific and the Philosophical Ideas of Man.................... 11
2. What is Man?... 13
   A. The Unity of the Human Being....................................... 14
   B. The Bipolarity of the Human Being: Individuality and
      Personality.. 15
3. The Human Person... 17
   A. Knowledge of the Truth... 18
   B. The Will, Love and Freedom... 22
4. The Person and Society 25

Chapter II. FREEDOM AND THE FREEDOMS 29
1. A Philosophy of Freedom... 29
2. The Freedom of Spontaneity 32
3. The Freedom of Choice 34
   A. The Existence of the Free Will..................................... 34
   B. The Nature of Free Will.. 35
4. The Conquest of Freedom 39

Chapter III. EDUCATION FOR FREEDOM..................................... 49
1. What is Education? 49
2. The Primary Goals of Education.. 53
   A. The Conquest of Internal Freedom 53
   B. The Development of the Person in the Social Sphere................. 60
3. Self-Education or Education by another?............................... 62

Chapter IV. EDUCATION: A HUMAN AWAKENING 67
1. The Direction and Basic Requirements of the Education Process ... 68
   A. The Existential Curve or Personal Awakening to the Values of
      Life: Existence, Work, Other persons 69
   B. The Sapiental Curve or the Love of Truth directed toward
      Wisdom 72
2. Educational Influences.. 78
   A. The Family 78
   B. The School 79
   C. The School of Life 81

Chapter V. THE SCHOOL AND LIBERAL EDUCATION 83
  1. To Educate or to Instruct 83
     A. The Appropriate Role of the School 83
     B. The Stages of School Education 85
  2. The Secondary School: Liberal Education for All 88
     A. The Maritainian Concept of the Humanities 89
     B. The Curriculum in Secondary Education 90
     C. The Discourse on Method of Secondary Education 93
  3. Advanced Studies and the Ideal University 96
     A. The Ideal University 98
     B. An Alternative 100
     C. Complements of University Education 101
  4. The School and Moral Education 102
     A. School Life 103
     B. The Teaching of Morality 103
     C. Pluralism in the School 105
  5. Christian Education 106
     A. The Curriculum of a Christian College 107
     B. The Development of Christian Intelligence 108
     C. The Means of Strengthening Spiritual Life 109

Chapter VI. THE RELEVANCE OF MARITAIN 111
  1. An Education for Freedom 111
  2. A Pedagogy for our Time 115
  3. A Source for Exploration 119

Bibliography 123

Translator's Forward

Any translation moves between literalness and literariness, absolute fidelity to the original and the reconstruction necessary to produce a work in conformity with the norms and usages of another language. The danger of literalness is to fall into unacceptable constructions (in this case Gallicisms). On the other hand, literariness risks imposing a form on thought which may not betray the meaning, but can falsify the tone or atmosphere of a work. I assume that in a translation of a philosophical work, like that of Allard, the aim must be precision and clarity, not the tranformation of the author through a style foreign to him. Unlike one of Maritain's translators who was fond of alliteration and on occasion presented the Parisian philosopher in the garments of *Piers Plowman,* I have sinned — if sin there be — on the side of literalness.

A decision was made to utilize the existing translations of Maritain's works, despite the obvious shortcomings of some. The misadventures associated with English versions of Maritain's work is a tale in itself, as witness the fact that two translations have been done of *Les degrés du savoir* and two of *Humanisme intégral.* However, changes have been made in some places. In all instances I have replaced speculative by theoretical. The use of speculative ignores the connotations which the term has in common speech. How can we escape from the stock market, on one hand, or the idea of undisciplined mind-spinning (which is the way the term is often conceived by social scientists) on the other? Neither theoretical nor theory carries such a weight of accumulated meaning. In the second case, one translation rendered *mobiles* as mobiles, in English a form of freely moving sculpture having nothing to do with the psychological elements indicated in the context. Otherwise the published translations are unaltered.

Finally, I trust that the English version will be an avenue to understanding Professor Allard's message, not a road block. Since that is my intention, any obscurities in the translation must be attributed to the translator. The original text is limpid.

Ralph C. Nelson,
University of Windsor.

Abbreviations Used

Most of the references to Jacques Maritain's works are made using the following abbreviations. The edition used in each case is the one indicated here (and in the bibliography).

ASE   *Approches sans entraves*, Fayard, 1973

BPT   *Bergsonian Philosophy and Thomism*, Philosophical Library, 1955

BT   *De Bergson à Thomas d'Aquin*, Hartmann, 1947

C   *Education at the Crossroads*, Yale University Press, 1943.

CD   *Christianity and Democracy*, Charles Scribner's Sons, 1944

CI   *Creative Intuition in Art and Poetry*, Pantheon Books, 1953

CN   *Carnet de notes*, Desclée de Brouwer, 1965

DD   *Dream of Descartes*, Philosophical Library, 1944

DK   *Distinguish to Unite, or The Degrees of Knowledge*, Charles Scribner's Sons, 1959

EE   *Existence and the Existent*, Pantheon Books, 1948

EM   *The Education of Man: The Educational Philosophy of Jacques Maritain*, Edited and with an Introduction by Donald and Idella Gallagher, 1963

ET   "Reflections on Necessity and Contingency," *Essays in Thomism*, Edited by Robert E. Brennan, Sheed and Ward, 1942

EW   "Confession of Faith," *The Social and Political Philosophy of Jacques Maritain*. Edited by Joseph W. Evans and Leo Ward, Charles Scribner's Sons, 1955.

F   "The Conquest of Freedom," *Freedom, Its Meaning*. Edited by Ruth N. Anshen, George Allen and Unwin, 1942

FMW   *Freedom in the Modern World*, Charles Scribner's Sons, 1936

IH   *Integral Humanism*, Charles Scribner's Sons, 1968

MS   *Man and the State*, University of Chicago Press, 1951

PCG   *The Person and the Common Good*, University of Notre Dame Press, 1966

PDC   *Le philosophe dans la cité*, Alsatia, 1960

PE   *Pour une philosophie de l'éducation*, Fayard, 1969

PG   *The Peasant of the Garonne*, Holt, Rinehart and Winston, 1968

PM   *A Preface to Metaphysics, Seven Lectures on Being*, Sheed and Ward, 1939

QC   *Questions de conscience*, Desclée de Brouwer, 1938

RC   *Religion and Culture*, Sheed and Ward, 1931

RI   *Réflexions sur l'intelligence et sur sa vie propre*, Nouvelle Librairie nationale, 1924

RM   *The Rights of Man and Natural Law*, Charles Scribner's Sons 1943

RR   *The Range of Reason*, Charles Scribner's Sons, 1952.

RT   *Ransoming the Time*, Charles Scribner's Sons, 1941

SH   *Le sort de l'homme*, Éditions de la Baconnière, 1943

SP   *Scholasticism and Politics*, Doubleday and Company, 1960

SW   *Science and Wisdom*, Charles Scribner's Sons, 1940

T   *Theonas: Conversations of a Sage*, Sheed and Ward, 1935.

TA   *Saint Thomas Aquinas*, Meridian Books, 1958

TR   *Three Reformers: Luther, Descartes, Rousseau*, Sheed and Ward, 1935

UP   *On the Use of Philosophy*, Princeton University Press, 1961

Introduction

More and more the history of mankind appears as the history of the progressive mastery of man over nature and the conquest of human autonomy. And man seems to have a more lively awareness of his freedom. "Ever since the French Revolution and the effusion of a secularized Christian idealism which it provoked in history, the sense of freedom and the sense of social justice have convulsed and vitalized our civilization" (CD, 22).

This meaning of freedom has preoccupied as well the world of education; suffice it to mention in this regard several striking examples, namely, the experiences of Neill at Summerhill,[1] the educational practice of Paulo Freire in the adult literacy campaign in Brazil,[2] and the debate over non-directivity in education.[3]

Thus the title of this study, *Education for Freedom,* corresponds to a fundamental problem in education; it brings to light an essential aspect of Jacques Maritain's educational thought. "Education directed toward wisdom, centered on the humanities, aiming to develop in people the capacity to think correctly and to enjoy truth and beauty, is education for freedom, or liberal education. Whatever his particular vocation may be, and whatever special training his vocation may require, every human being is entitled to receive such a properly human and humanistic education" (EM, 69).

This expression, *Education for Freedom,* is adopted from the title of a work by Robert Hutchins, a friend of Jacques Maritain, in which the author stresses the need for a spiritual revolution in education and shows the primary role of the humanities — the liberal arts — in this revolution.[4] In his book

---

[1] A.S. NEILL, *Summerhill* (Harmondsworth: Penguin, 1971).

[2] Paulo FREIRE, *Education for Critical Consciousness,* translated from Brazilian (New York: Seabury Press, 1973).

[3] Georges SNYDERS, *Où vont les pédagogies non-directives?* Third edition (Paris: Presses Universitaires de France, 1975). Moreover there is apparently increasing uncertainty about non-directive education as the recent work of Daniel HAMELINE and Marie-Joëlle DARDELIN, *La liberté d'apprendre,* Situation II (Paris: Les Editions ouvrières, 1977), testifies.

[4] Robert M. HUTCHINS, *Education for Freedom* (Baton Rouge: Louisiana State University Press, 1943).

> The alternatives before us are clear. Either we must abandon the ideal of freedom or we must educate our people for freedom. If an education in the liberal arts and in the great books is the education for freedom, then we must make the attempt to give this education to all our citizens. *Ibid.,* pp. 17-18.

Brave New World Revisited, Aldous Huxley points out what he considers to be future paths in education in a chapter entitled, *Education for Freedom:* "such an education for freedom should be, as I have said, an education first of all in facts and in values — the facts of individual diversity and genetic uniqueness and the values of freedom, tolerance and mutual charity which are the ethical corollaries of these facts."[5]

In this study, it is our intention to set forth the main lines of Maritain's educational thought in the hope that his philosophy of education will stimulate our minds — and enlighten them as well — to the challenges raised by contemporary education, where it becomes increasingly evident that "man no longer believes that science and technology alone insure the progress and happiness of his species" (PDC, 49).

By way of introduction, we will give a brief sketch of Maritain the philosopher and then examine his works on the philosophy of education.

I.- JACQUES MARITAIN, THOMISTIC PHILOSOPHER

Professor Fernand Brunner, in his opening address to the 16th Congress of French-speaking philosophy associations in 1974, eulogized Maritain in the following terms:

> Jacques Maritain, who died last year at the age of ninety-two, taught at the Catholic Institute of Paris, Princeton and Columbia, and filled the post of French Ambassador to the Vatican. His work represents an important tendency in Neo-Thomism — he prefered to say he was just a Thomist — and showed his ambition to extract the thought of Thomas Aquinas from its theological gangue in order to consider it as philosophy.
>
> For many of our members Maritain's name summons up the idea of a closed and rigid orthodoxy. But they overlook the fact that this philosophy of being is open to modern problems and that Maritain's thought fits into the contemporary problematic through his criticisms of Bergsonism and Existentialism and by his moral and political reflections and his reflections on art which remains one of his greatest achievements. The philosopher would consider *Creative Intuition* as his most successful work.
>
> Maritain has had disciples and has affected men's souls and that counts for a lot. In lively and pure meditations, already beginning a few years after he was converted at the age of twenty-four, Maritain, far from the cult of the fashionable, continuously enriched the French philosophical tradition with his great work.[6]

This is, or appears to be a paradoxical kind of eulogy. An "orthodox" Thomistic philosopher and yet one open to modern problems; a mode of thought medieval in origin, but fitting into the contemporary problematic! Yet this is precisely what Maritain tried to achieve, believing himself justified to consider his thought as both anti and ultramodern.[7]

"Woe is me if I do not Thomisticize," he wrote in one of his first books. "And through thirty years of work and struggle I have proceeded along the same path with the feeling of sympathizing all the more deeply with the

---

    [5]   Aldous HUXLEY, *Brave New World Revisited* (London: Chatto and Windus, 1959), p. 145.

    [6]   Fernand BRUNNER, Chairman, Opening Address in *Actes du XVIe Congrès des Sociétés de philosophie de langue française* (Reims, September 3-6, 1974, *La Culture,* Vander-Nauwelaerts, 1975), p. 5.

    [7]   "What I call antimodern here could just as well be called ultramodern," *Antimoderne* (Paris: Editions de la Revue des jeunes, 1922), p. 14. *Ibid.:* "Vae mihi, si non thomistizavero."

searchings, discoveries and anxieties of modern thought as I tried to make the light, which comes to us from a wisdom elaborated by the ages and resisting the flux of time, diffuse further into it'' (PDC, 24). In fact, Maritain considers Thomistic philosophy not as a system, but as a spiritual organism, as ''an essentially progressive and assimilative doctrine'' (DK, xiii). It is a philosophy of being in which the aspect of mystery is naturally predominant. ''The mystery we conclude is a fullness of being with which the intellect enters into a vital union and into which it plunges without exhausting it. Could it do so it would be God, *ipsum Esse subsistens* and the author of being. The Supreme 'mystery' is the supernatural mystery which is the object of faith and theology. [...]. But philosophy and science also are concerned with mystery, another mystery, the mystery of nature and the mystery of being. A philosophy unaware of mystery would not be a philosophy'' (PM, 4-5).

This is why Thomistic philosophy should not be seen as a compendium of knowledge encompassing the answers to all questions, ''this would be a great stupidity'' (PG, 96). Indeed Maritain sees in Thomism a true philosophy, but one as unfinished as is the reality which it reflects. ''Authentic Thomism is always anxious to discover, acknowledge and integrate new truths. It strives to manufacture a key that opens, not closes doors. By the very fact that it is a doctrine in movement and vital development, it is not a closed system, but an essentially open wisdom without limits'' (ASE, 68). It is open to new questions as it is to what can be salvaged from cultural and scientific evolution; it is open to the contributions, problematics and basic insights of philosophies which appear in every age; ''above all it is an insatiable hunger and quenchless thirst for truth to be grasped and assimilated'' (ASE, 69).

Thus, according to Maritain, we should not take Thomism for a garment worn in the thirteenth century and no longer in style; the philosophical thought of Saint Thomas Aquinas is the fruition of labours preceding it and must be enriched by those which have followed since. A collection of true principles organically interconnected in conformity with reality is the heritage of this long tradition, and this heritage enables the mind of the philosopher to advance from age to age toward an increase in truth, presupposing an infinity of truths not yet attained, implying the possibility of error, and requiring a constant review of one's own ideas along with the duty to understand other philosophical teachings.

All too briefly and imperfectly sketched, such is the way in which Maritain has understood and explained the adjective *Thomistic* that he assigns to his philosophy.

II.- JACQUES MARITAIN, CHRISTIAN PHILOSOPHER

Along with Gilson, Blondel and Brunschvicq, Jacques Maritain took part in the famous debate of the Thirties on Christian philosophy and he explained his views on this difficult and thorny question on a number of occasions in his writings.[8]

---

[8] See especially *An Essay on Christian Philosophy* (New York: Philosophical Library, 1955) and *Science and Wisdom* (London: Geoffrey Bles, 1954).

To begin with let us note that the expression Christian philosophy seemed ambiguous to him. "How can I do otherwise than use the expression Christian philosophy? To tell the truth, I am scarcely enchanted by it. There comes a moment when all phrases seem to betray, and this phrase runs the risk of calling up in the mind (in the mind of those who are prejudiced, and we are all so) a sort of crossing or attenuation of philosophy by Christianity, a sort of enrolling of philosophy in a pious confraternity or a bon dévot parti" (SW, 136). In fact this expression can only be used in a "material sense" to designate western philosophy even when that philosophy betrays Christian thought, for its themes are inspired by this thought. If philosophy is considered in its "formal sense", it is an activity of natural reason properly speaking and so no more Christian than pagan; by its own nature, philosophy "depends only on the evidence and criteria of natural reason" (SW, 138).

However, the philosophical act is the act of a human person who, in fact, can be pre-Christian, Christian or non-Christian; as a consequence, and without changing its intrinsic nature, this philosophical act is in a pre-Christian, Christian or non-Christian "state" depending on the particular case. Definite tensions can result from these situations. For instance, the Christian philosopher can and even ought to philosophize by taking into account the contribution of his faith. Tensions can also rise between Christian philosophers and non-Christian ones; an attempt should be made to lessen these tensions and overcome the mutual distrust which they breed without forgetting that agreement among philosophers will never be completely achieved, for "the natural condition of any philosopher seems to imply he can be in agreement only with himself. Even this kind of agreement seems rather difficult and due to some infrequent kind of luck[9]."

Maritain appraises Thomistic philosophy in the light of this distinction between the nature of philosophy and its state: "Taken by itself philosophy is based and achieves stability only on pure intelligible necessities imposing themselves on reason. Perfectly distinct from theology whose object is revealed data, philosophy's own fulcrum is in no way religious belief, but the evidence of the object alone and the adherence of the intellect to all that reality which can be grasped naturally. Thomistic philosophy is valuable as philosophy not because it is Christian, but because it is demonstrably true. Aristotle, its first founder, was no Christian...''[10]

III.- MARITAIN, PHILOSOPHER OF BEING

Maritain then is a Thomistic and Christian philosopher, but if the meaning he gives to these two adjectives were well understood, it would probably be more correct to see in him a philosopher in the full sense of the word who is certainly inspired by the principles of Aristotle and Saint Thomas Aquinas, who recognizes the "objective state" and "subjective reinforcements" of the Christian faith, but who strives above all to respond to the very

---

[9]   "About Christian Philosophy", in Barduin V. SCHWARZ (ed.), *The Human Person and the World of Values* (New York: Fordham University Press, 1960), p. 10.
[10]   "Le thomisme et la civilisation", in *Revue de Philosophie,* 1928, p. 110.

requirements of philosophical reflection.[11] "The philosopher swears fidelity to no person, nor any school — not even, if he is a Thomist, to the letter of St. Thomas and every article of his teaching. He is surely in need of teachers and of a tradition, but in order for them to teach him to think when he looks at things (which is not as simple as all that), and not, as is the case with the theologian, so that he can assume the whole of this tradition into his thought. Once this tradition has instructed him, he is free of it and makes use of it for his own work. In this case, he is alone in the face of being; for his job is to think over that which is" (PG, 137).

Thus, Maritain is a philosopher of being, meaning a philosopher paying heed to existence in its richness and in its diversity, evidently presupposing that he is a realist. "Christianity professes with a tranquil impudence what in the philosophical vocabulary is known as realism. I said previously that a Christian cannot be a relativist. One must say, and this goes much further, that a Christian cannot be an idealist" (PG, 100).[12]

And then the philosophical work is "dependent for its principles and structure on experience and reason" (TA, xiii). The intellect or reason at issue here is not the understanding in the Cartesian sense nor in the Kantian sense; it is a perceptive power in the fullest sense of the term having its proper object, even if it is rooted in sense knowledge; consequently philosophy "proceeds from the visible to the invisible, I mean to what is of itself outside the order of sensible observation (for the simple reason that the principles which he reaches are in themselves pure objects of understanding and not objects of sensible apprehension or imaginative representation). Here is a world unimaginable by nature, or 'negatively' " (DK, 47).

This philosophy of being expressed in different "degrees of knowledge" is both ancient and modern, it develops progressively by a process of deepening. For if man the metaphysical animal "cannot dispense with the absolute" (RI, 303), metaphysics remains an extremely difficult venture of the mind and "the gods are jealous of our joy in it" (DD, 68). Moreover, all philosophers contribute to this deepening in a variety of ways. "With every great philosopher and every great thinker there is a central intuition which in itself does not mislead" (RT, 60). And this intuition is an enhancement of the philosophy of being, the *philosophia perennis:* "Finally philosophers quarrel so violently because each one has seen some truth which, more often than not, has dazzled his eyes, and which he may conceptualize in an erroneous

---

[11] "He is widely regarded as the pre-eminent modern interpreter of the thought of St. Thomas Aquinas and as a highly creative thinker in his own right." "Maritain's thought is based on the principles of Aristotle and St. Thomas, but incorporates many insights found in other philosophers, both classical and modern, and also profits greatly from data supplied by such sciences of man as anthropology, sociology, and psychology." Joseph W. EVANS, Introduction, *Jacques Maritain, The Man and His Achievement* (New York: Sheed and Ward, 1963), pp. IX and XI.

[12] "A knowledge that despises what is, is itself nothing; a cherry between the teeth holds within it more mystery than the whole of idealist metaphysics". *Distinguish to Unite, Or the Degrees of Knowledge* (London: Geoffrey Bles, 1959), p. 335.

manner, but of which his fellow-philosophers must also be aware, each in his own perspective" (UP, 6).[13]

For Maritain, the philosophy of being (or Thomism) "is not a school or museum philosophy, but an open air philosophy in which concrete experience, constantly renewed, plays a primary role. It is a philosophy which presupposes both the strong foundation of common sense and fidelity to intellectual insight as complete as that of true poetry to creative intuition. It is a philosophy nourished on the inheritance of a long tradition, but nourished so as to enter all the more forcibly into the problems of the age and advance toward novelties with composure and boldness. Its' ambition is to provide a voice in the chorus (I didn't say the discord, I said the chorus) for any strivings after truth, from whatever region or system it originates."[14]

The young Maritain, combining with the fervour of a neophyte new and old things, antimodern and ultramodern, was so intransigeant that the negative reactions his thought provoked can be easily understood.[15] But a close reading of his work allows us to comprehend the honest effort he expended to be receptive to other philosophers and other philosophies, without sacrificing in any way what he believed to be true.

In his *Letter to Jean Cocteau* in 1926, Maritain describes very well what he has tried to do as a philosopher, his philosophical ideal. It would be worthwhile reading an extract of this letter before presenting of Maritain's work in the philosophy of education:

> I have been riveted to the most dogmatic, keenest thought, the least capable of conciliation and softening, to a doctrine that is absolutely hard, in order to try, while contemplating our times as they pass, not to scatter but to take on, to reconcile. The fact is, I have confidence in the truth. As universal as being, truth must gather everywhere the fragments snatched from unity; she alone can do it. Minds recognize each other only in the light; the purer it is, the more it is divided from the shadows, the more it unites.
>
> I had to start out with controversy; it bores me more and more... Our business is to find the positive in all things; to use what is true less to strike than to cure. There is so little

---

[13] "In metaphysics and philosophy, where the 'mystery' aspect is predominant, progress takes place chiefly by deeper penetration. Besides, the different philosophical systems, however ill founded they may be, constitute in some way, in their totality, a virtual and fluent philosophy, overlapping contrary formulations and unfriendly doctrines and carried along by the elements of truth they contain." "Confession of Faith", Joseph EVANS and Leo WARD, *The Social and Political Philosophy of Jacques Maritain. Selected Readings* (New York: Charles Scribner's Sons, 1955), p. 333.

[14] J. MARITAIN, preface in Henry BARS, *La politique selon Jacques Maritain* (Paris: Les Editions Ouvrières, 1961), p. 13.

[15] "You know that in my youth I spend some years breaking windows, and afterwards I tried as best I could to open doors, and to open paths." *God and the Permission of Evil* (Milwaukee: The Bruce Publishing Company, 1966), p. 113. "At this period in 1908 I imagined that the essential task of philosophy was to refute error. I have made some headway since then. I have come to understand that refutation is only a secondary job and most often vain and useless (and it has been terribly damaging for Thomism). One should not be refuting but 'clarifying and moving ahead. (A note written in 1954.) *Carnet de Notes* (Paris: Desclée de Brouwer, 1965), p. 69.
"*Nova et vetera* — new things and old things — and the 'new' growing out of the 'old' — this is Maritain's style as a philosopher." Joseph W. EVANS, "Jacques Maritain", in *The New Scholasticism,* Maritain's Ninetieth Birthday, Vol. XLVI, 1972, p. 6.

love in the world; men's hearts are so cold, so frozen, even in people who are right — the only ones who could help the others. One must have a hard mind and a meek heart.[16]

IV.- MARITAIN, PHILOSOPHER OF EDUCATION

Maritain has examined a large number of philosophical questions in his work, both vast and extremely varied, ranging from logic to metaphysics, the philosophy of nature to the philosophy of knowledge, moral philosophy to political philosophy, the philosophy of culture to the philosophy of history. It seems natural to him that a philosophy of being could deal with questions related to the different analogues of being and the different manifestations or "epiphanies" of being and especially of its many-faceted expressions in the human being, while taking into account his present situation. Thomism "answers modern problems, both theoretical and practical. In face of contemporary aspirations and perplexities, it displays a power to fashion and emancipate the mind. We therefore look to Thomism at the present day to save, in the theoretical order, intellectual values, in the practical order, so far as they can be saved by philosophy, human values" (PM, 1).

It is not surprising to discover that "the philosophical work of Jacques Maritain tends completely toward the advancement of what is human in man and in society" (PE,).[17] Isn't man the principal subject of philosophy? That is why the philosophy of being, becomes with Maritain, by a quite natural development, a philosophy of the person and mind. "So," as Olivier Lacombe correctly writes, "Jacques Maritain has always taught that the philosophy of being, reaching completion in a realist theory of knowledge, establishes the true philosophy of the subject, to which he has devoted a good deal of effort and some of his finest pages. When the subject arrives at consciousness and freedom and relives the dignity of the person, it doesn't place itself beyond or on the edge of being, but achieves its highest advancement."[18]

In this personalist perspective, it was fitting that Maritain became interested in the problems and philosophy of education. Moreover this interest in education was evident at an early age. The young Maritain, who was only sixteen, wrote in a letter to François Baton in 1898: "And of course all that I shall think and know, I shall devote to the cause of the proletariat and to

---

[16] *Art and Faith,* Letters between Jacques Maritain and Jean Cocteau (New York: Philosophical Library, 1948), p. 114. In *Approches sans entraves* (Paris: Fayard, 1973), Maritain writes: "In a fraternal dialogue, the deeper love is, the more each one must declare without extenuation what he holds to be true (if he doesn't he not only inflicts an injury on the truth such as he sees it, but also on the spiritual dignity of his neighbor).

And the more freely I assert what I hold to be true, the more I must love the person who denies it (for truly I do not have the tolerance for my neighbor required by fraternal charity unless his right to exist, to seek the truth and express it according to his lights is acknowledged and respected by me at the very moment that my neighbor takes sides against the truths which I hold dearest)" (p. 61).

[17] Editor's note in *Pour une philosophie de l'éducation,* p. 9.

[18] Olivier LACOMBE, "Jacques Maritain et la philosophie de l'être", in *Les Etudes philosophiques,* January-March, 1972, p. 72. "Thus, 'philosophy of being' is at once, and *par excellence,* 'philosophy of mind"" (DK, p. IX).

mankind; I shall use it completely for the preparation of the revolution and the education of mankind'' (CN, 17).

But it was not until 1927 that Maritain's first text on education appeared in the preface to the French edition of a book by Franz de Hovre, *Essai de philosophie pédagogique*. In this preface, Maritain articulates the two leading ideas of his educational thought: firstly, the primary role of philosophy in the realm of educational thought;[19] secondly, the important contribution that Thomistic philosophy could bring to the philosophy of education.[20]

The French philosopher expounded his ideas on education in America in a series of lectures (The Terry Lectures) delivered at Yale University in 1943. These lectures were published the same year under the title, *Education at the Crossroads*.[21] Maritain deals with moral education less than two years later in 1945.[22] In 1952, he adds a lecture on "Education and the Humanities", given at Saint Michael's College in Toronto. Maritain set out his views on education in synthetic form in an essay entitled "Thomist Views on Education", written in 1955 for the collection *Modern Philosophies and Education*.[23]

Two other papers followed, namely "On Some Typical Aspects of Christian Education" (a discourse delivered at a seminar on education at Kent School), and "Moral and Spiritual Values in Education", a lecture given in 1958.

In 1959, Maritain published his most important texts on the philosophy of education for his French readers; this book entitled *Pour une philosophie de l'éducation* brought together the following texts: *Education at the Crossroads*, "Thomist Views on Education", "On Some Typical Aspects of Christian Education", to which was added, in an appendix, an original essay on the problem of public schools in France.[24] A new edition of this work, revised and completed, appeared in 1969. The other texts of Maritain can be found in a work published by Professors Donald and Idella Gallagher, *The Education of Man*.[25]

At first glance, his philosophy of education might appear of relatively little importance in comparison with the corpus of Maritain's philosophical work. Yet a study of his thought on the subject quickly convinces us that what

---

[19]   "Every theory of education is based on a conception of life and, consequently, is associated necessarily with a system of philosophy." Preface to French Edition of *Philosophy and Education*, New York: Benziger Brothers, 1931, p. VI. "What does this means if not that education is by nature a function of philosophy, of metaphysics? 'There is no such thing as neutral education; either it is not neutral or it is not education'" (*Ibid.*, p. VII).

[20]   *Ibid.*, p. IX-X.

[21]   *Education at the Crossroads* (New Haven: Yale University Press, 1943).

[22]   "Moral Education" in *A College goes to School: Centennial Lectures* (Notre Dame and Holy Cross, Indiana: St. Mary's College, and Paterson, New Jersey: St. Anthony Guild Press, 1945), pp. 1-25.

[23]   "Thomist Views on Education", in *Modern Philosophies and Education*, edited by Nelson B. Henry (Chicago: University of Chicago Press, 1955), pp. 57-90.

[24]   *Pour une philosophie de l'éducation* (Paris: Fayard, 1959).

[25]   *The Education of Man, The Educational Philosophy of Jacques Maritain*, Edited and with an Introduction by Donald and Idella GALLAGHER (Notre Dame: Notre Dame University Press, 1963).

is at stake is a coherent philosophy, a dynamic continuation of his metaphysics and enhanced with contributions from other philosophies of education.

Charles Journet, a great friend of Maritain, wrote concerning *Education at the Crossroads:*

> When we glanced for the first time on *Education at the Crossroads* — it happened in Rome in October, 1945 — we had the impression of finally discovering, in the first few chapters, the small treatise on education, based on the data of Saint Augustine and Saint Thomas Aquinas that we were seeking for a long time. We were immediately struck by the exceptional soundness of the distinctions set forth in it, the fecundity of its insights, the clarity of its definitions, the wealth of solutions that it brought to the questions so often asked, and above all its mastery of shortcuts and the perfectly simple way in which the author touched on the most crucial issues.[26]

The editor's note in the second edition of *Pour une philosophie de l'éducation* pertinently recalls to the reader the fact that "these are not just proposals, or occasional lectures, hastily thrown together; one draws out of these texts an ordered and complete whole" (PE, 9). In this respect the judgment of Donald and Idella Gallagher reflects quite well an opinion shared by many American philosophers: "The philosophy of education issuing from this half century of teaching, and from meditating upon the principles of education and the practical problems involved in schooling the young, is undoubtedly one of the lasting contributions of this eminent Thomist to twentieth-century thought."[27]

We have decided to follow the order of the internal development of his philosophy in the present work devoted to Maritain's educational thought.

Maritain asserts that "the prime goal of education is the conquest of internal and spiritual freedom to be achieved by the individual person, or, in other words, his liberation through knowledge and wisdom, good will, and love" (C, 11). If it is the case that "every theory of education is based on a conception of life and, consequently, is associated necessarily with a system of philosophy",[28] it would appear that the Maritainean conception of education is based on a philosophy of freedom,[29] which implies a philosophy of the person, whose proper act is precisely the free one; freedom "cannot be constituted unless its author is first able to answer the question: What is man? Why was he made? What is the end of human life" (FMW, 14).

So, the sequence of chapters will be in the following order. First, we will present the fundamental articulations of Maritain's personalism and his philosophy of man, and we will stress the basic distinction between individual and person.

Secondly, we will reveal the different meanings of the word freedom, namely the freedom of choice and that of spontaneity which will allow us to

---

[26] Charles JOURNET, Forward to the French edition of *Education at the Crossroads* in *Pour une philosophie de l'éducation* (1959 edition), p. 14.

[27] Donald and Idella GALLAGHER, Introduction, *The Education of Man*, p. 9.

[28] Preface to the French Edition in Franz DE HOVRE, *Philosophy and Education*, p. VI.

[29] A list of the principal texts of Maritain on freedom will be presented in the first part of the bibliography.

understand in a better way the direction of human freedom, its dynamism starting with the minimal freedom and leading up to freedom of expansion or perfection.

Then we shall be in a position to study the central theme of Maritain's philosophy of education (in Chapters III and IV) by scrutinizing in turn the question of purposes in education and of educational dynamics.

In the fifth chapter, we intend to analyze the role of the school particularly that of the secondary school which should offer a "liberal education for all"; in that chapter we shall study as well the difficult question of religious and moral education.

We shall conclude our study by trying to underline Maritain's contribution to the pedagogy of our time.

Chapter I

Maritain's Personalism

I.- THE SCIENTIFIC AND THE PHILOSOPHICAL IDEAS OF MAN

"If the aim of education is the helping and guiding of man toward his own human achievement, education cannot escape the problems and entanglements of philosophy, for it supposes by its very nature a philosophy of man, and from the outset it is obliged to answer the question: 'What is man?' which the philosophical sphinx is asking" (C, 4). In fact, the idea one has of man is fundamental in education, for education is an art. An art is defined by its purpose: "Art's very vitality is the energy with which it tends toward its end, without stopping at any intermediary step" (C, 3). For, the aim of education — the art of all arts — is to encourage the emergence of man, to give birth to the human. That is why any educational art bears within it a conception of man, and it cannot remain neutral in this regard.[1]

In like manner, every age of mankind manifests one or many models of man which it has borne: "Every great cultural period is dominated by a special idea that man has of himself. It is a privilege of the intellect that we contemplate in the mirror of our ever changing knowledge 'the face of our birth', and as much as they depend on our nature itself, so do our activity and life depend on this image of our nature" (RI, 292). Maritain is not indulgent for our age of scientific progress which, in spite of its promise of human liberation, actually leads to a debasement of what is human; he goes along on this issue with the constellation of existential and personalist thinkers and others who have expressed serious misgivings and severe criticisms about the invasion of technology and about positivism. "Today human dignity is everywhere trampled down. Still more, it crumbles from within, for in the mere perspective of science and technology, we are at a loss to discover the rational foundations of the dignity of the human person and to believe in it.

---

[1] "An educational theory is necessarily normative. However it is stated, it sets out to define and to realize an ideal. But any definition of such an ideal is, in turn, necessarily tied to an attitude in regard to human nature. One may think that education should conform to the teachings of nature, or, on the contrary, one may consider the rationale of education to be the modification of nature. In any case, an educational theory requires beforehand a reflection on man considered in his actual being and in his vocation." Jacques ULMANN, *La nature et l'éducation* (Paris: Vrin, 1964), p. 7.

The task of the mergent civilization (which will doubtless not appear tomorrow but which may possibly appear the day after tomorrow), will consist in refinding and refounding the sense of that dignity, in rehabilitating man..." (RR, 93).

Maritain's criticisms do not strike at the progress made by the sciences in themselves but rather at the tendency of scientific forms of knowledge toward monopoly in our technological age. He recognizes without any difficulty the value of scientific conquests; for instance, he wrote in regard to the psychologists: "it would be ridiculous to underestimate the value of their work, and I have no intention of falling into this error. I have a good deal of admiration for Freud, if not for the Freudians, and I heartily value the discoveries of contemporary psychology, however incomplete" (PG, 153). "For science is good and worthy of love..." (SW, 18), and "the scientific improvement of the pedagogical means and methods is in itself outstanding progress. But the more it takes on importance, the more it requires a parallel strengthening of practical wisdom and of the dynamic trend toward the goal" (C, 3-4).[2]

Of course science can furnish — and does furnish — precious information concerning the means and instruments which is incessantly renewed; but its radical inadequacy results from the fact that "the purely scientific idea of man is, and must be, a phenomenalized idea without reference to ultimate reality" (C, 5).[3] Hence it can't supply us with anything about the foundations of education, about its purpose, for it cannot make statements about what man is nor about values.[4] That is why the scientific idea of man, taken exclusively, would falsify the idea of man and the idea of his education, by becoming, so to speak, a substitute for metaphysics. Such is the meaning of the criticism of Freudian *philosophy* made by Maritain: "Nothing is more unpleasant than to speak of a philosophy which does not recognize itself as such. The whole of Freudian philosophy is based upon a prejudice: the violent negation of spirituality and liberty. Experimental views, which are often correct, become philosophically hardened, and transform themselves into the worst errors" (SP, 157).

---

[2] "If not in its nature, at least in its human dynamism and in its relation to human life, it (science) belongs to the sphere of *uti,* and it is absurd to take the useful as end. An end is that which is truly ultimate and delectable, and wisdom belongs to the order of *frui*" (SW, 18).

[3] "On the other hand, Kantian criticism has shown that the science of phenomena brings with it no instrument capable of discovering for us the thing in itself, the cause of its ontological reality. And Kant saw very well the incapacity of an experimental and scientific equipment to reach over to metaphysics, or more generally to ontology, to philosophical knowledge. His error consisted in making a false generalisation from this partial view — for he, too, idolized the science of his time — and building on it his philosophy of knowledge" (SW, 44-45).

[4] "This inadequacy of the 'sciences' in so far as sciences is not provisional but permanent, not just contingent, but necessary. It is forever and intrinsically that the organization of education does not depend only on the sciences. Even in their most polished form, supposing them to have attained the highest point of their ascent, the positive sciences remain unqualified to prescribe values." Guy AVANZINI, *Introduction aux sciences de l'éducation* (Toulouse: Privat, 1976), p. 106.

Olivier Reboul rightly states that the philosophy of education "confronts us with the most radical question: what is man that he has to be educated?"[5] and he asserts that any attempt to answer this philosophical inquiry is rooted in metaphysical assumptions. In contrast to the phenomenalized or scientific idea of man, and complementing it, Maritain offers an ontological conception of man, a conception bearing on the intrinsic characteristics of a human being, his intelligible density, inaccessible to sense knowledge as such.

II.- WHAT IS MAN?

"In answer to our question, then, 'What is man?', we may give the Greek, Jewish, and Christian idea of man: man as an animal endowed with reason, whose supreme dignity is the intellect; and man as a free individual in personal relation with God, whose supreme righteousness consists in voluntarily obeying the law of God; and man as a sinful and wounded creature called to divine life and to the freedom of grace, whose supreme perfection consists of love" (C, 7).

This idea of man is set forth by Maritain as the basis of his philosophy of education because he holds it to be the true one; but he also notes that our civilization is permeated by it and that "in fact man in our civilization is a more or less secularized version of the Christian man". As a consequence, this philosophical and religious idea of man can serve as a common basis for a lot of thinkers whose metaphysics or religious belief is in a community of analogy with it, for instance, the great metaphysical systems which recognize the dignity of the spirit, different forms of Christian and Judaic belief, and also other religious beliefs, which recognize the divine destiny of man.

"In a Judeo-Greco-Christian civilization like ours, this community of analogy, which extends from the most orthodox religious forms of thought to the mere humanistic ones, makes it possible for a Christian philosophy of education, if it is well founded and rationally developed, to play an inspiring part in the concert, even for those who do not share in the creed of its supporters" (C, 7). Of course an exception has to be made — and Maritain willingly concurs — of those who adhere to completely opposed conceptions such as "materialistic metaphysics, positivism, or skepticism — I am not speaking here of Fascist and racist creeds, which do not belong at all in the civilized world" (C, 6).

In the following pages, it will be our concern to recall the elements of Maritain's philosophy of man by trying to show that this philosophy is, in line with the intention of its author, "well founded and rationally developed".

---

[5]   Olivier REBOUL, *La philosophie de l'éducation* (Paris: PUF, 1976), p. 6. "As a matter of fact a philosophy of education always depends on the metaphysical premises of its author" (*ibid.*, p. 10).

A. The Unity of the Human Being

The first part of the definition of man proposed by Maritain clearly indicates its Aristotelian origin: "man is an animal endowed with reason...",[6] that is to say a *material being* like all the animals, a being having a substantial unity like all material beings.

According to Aristotelian hylomorphism, every material being is *a substance,* composed of two substantial co-principles, namely: prime matter, the root of quantity, and the substantial form, the first substantial act and the root of qualitative determinations; so the human being is a composite substance, like other bodies (living or non-living) and is distinguished from them by the specific kind of substantial form which constitutes man in his own being. This is why "Thomist philosophy lays stress on the basic psychosomatic unity of the human being (one single substance composed of matter and a spirtual form or entelechy), thus affording us a philosophical key for a sound interpretation of great modern discoveries in neurology and psychiatry" (EM, 52).

Indeed by reason of his own nature, of his specific substantial form, man is also spirit while being a corporeal being. "Man is a metaphysical being, an animal that nourishes its life on transcendental things. There is no ethics among ants any more than among the stars; the road they are to follow is traced out for them in advance. But we men, merely because we know the sense of the word Being and of the word Why, and because into our poor head the whole heavens (and more than the heavens) can be fitted we are lost before we take our first step. We must lay out the road we follow; we must deliberate our end" (FMW, 14-15).

There is then a kind of duality in man, melded in a single substance: "a rational animal is, in the words of Saint Thomas, like a horizon between two worlds. He draws and carries the dark energies of the senses and instinct, of vegetal impulsion and matter to their culmination. And by his principal part he lives in the manner of a spirit, he has the eminent dignity of being a person master of his actions" (RI, 329-330).

The recognition of the spirituality of the human soul, of its transcendent character, is based, according to Maritain, on the facts of human experience: the fact of intellectual knowledge and the fact of human freedom being the principal manifestations of this spirituality. But the human soul is no less for that — quite the contrary — the substantial form of the human being, the first principle of its substantial unity: "According to this doctrine, the human soul, together with the matter which it informs, constitutes one substance, which is both carnal and spiritual. The soul is not, as Descartes believed, a thing — thought — existing on its own as a complete being, and the body another thing — extension — existing on its own as a complete being. Soul and matter

---

[6] "What is man for Aristotle and Saint Thomas? A rational animal. As a rational animal, man is by definition the most perfect of the animals and the most imperfect of the spirits." Jacques MARITAIN, "Le thomisme et la civilisation", *Revue de philosophie,* Volume XXXV, 1928, p. 116.

are the two substantial co-principles of the same being, of one and the same reality, called man. Because each soul is intended to animate a particular body, which receives its matter from the germinal cells, with all their hereditary content, from which it develops, and because, further, each soul has or is a substantial relation to a particular body, it has within its very substance the individual characteristics, which differentiate it from every other human soul" (PCG, 36).

This primary affirmation of the fundamental unity[7] of the human being is in contrast then with the Cartesian dualism.[8] On the other hand, the duality inscribed at the very heart of human existence — the existence of a composite substance — makes the realization of human becoming of which each free being and the society must share the responsibility both more difficult and more precarious: "Yet, man is flesh and spirit, not held together by a thread, but substantially united. The fact that human affairs cease to be cut to the measure of man (since some of those affairs take their rhythm from the energies of matter, while others look for their standards to the exigencies of a disincarnate spirituality) constitutes for man a frightful metaphysical disjunction. It is quite believable that the shape of this world will pass away on the day that this tension becomes so great that our heart will break" (DK, 15).

B. THE BIPOLARITY OF THE HUMAN BEING: INDIVIDUALITY AND PERSONALITY

Maritain's personalism expresses the effort expended by a philosophy of Thomistic inspiration[9] not only in order to prevent this splitting of modern

---

[7] "Now that man is a unity is a fact that must be accepted as such by the philosopher and placed beyond all discussion, or, what comes to the same thing, taken as the basis of any metaphysical theory. In order that the formulation of the problem be made completely clear, the following should still be added. It goes without saying that man cannot be reduced to his body, that he does not have the body of a brute animal. The important point is to show that he is not to be reduced to his soul, that the soul is not the man. Thus the burden of proof rests rather on an extreme spiritualism than on materialism." Roger VERNEAUX, *Philosophie de l'homme* (Paris: Beauchesne, 1956), p. 179.

[8] "If the spiritual and subsistent soul is the unique and substantial form of the human substance, and if man is not made up of two juxtaposed essences (as Cartesian spiritualism would have it, to the misfortune of modern thought); if man is a single natural whole — biological, sentient, rational — in virtue of the actuation of 'materia prima' by a form which is a spirit, the reason is that form (like essence) of itself implies a relationship to existence *(esse per se convenit formae)* and that it ought not to be conceived only as that by which a subject possesses in its essence such-and-such intelligible determinations, but also as that by which it is determinately constituted for existing and receives from its causes existential actuations" (EE, 38-39).

[9] The excellent study by Jacques CROTEAU on *Les fondements thomistes du personnalisme de Maritain* (Ottawa: Editions de l'Université d'Ottawa, 1955) seems to have established beyond any doubt the Thomistic inspiration of Maritain while reproaching him with using a terminology which does not correspond to that of the Angelic Doctor. "No doubt Saint Thomas doesn't group around the individual pole the relations of man-part with the common good, but the realities, covered by a similar terminology, undoubtedly are the same as those found in Saint Thomas' work under the term part" (p. 204). "Let us transfer to the name of part what Maritain attributes to individuality and we shall have a formulation of reality which conforms to the letter of Saint Thomas" (p. 218).

"Maritain's personalism can be dissociated from the distinction of individual and person while keeping its Thomistic character, because the person truly contains the formalities of whole man,[10] but especially to promote the harmonious development of the human being and to point out the paths of freedom and social liberation. At the core of this personalism "the metaphysical distinction between individuality and personality" (PCG, 13) is found.[11] Individuality constitutes the material pole of the human being, personality its spiritual pole.

Only individual realities exist. Pure spirits are individuals by reason of their form; that is why each individual is a particular species. But material beings are individuated through their matter, thus each human being is individuated by matter. Therefore he is a material individual, which means he is a part of the physical world subject to its laws, living by the senses and instinct (as well as by reason) (C, 9).

"So that in so far as we are individuals we are only a fragment of matter, a part of the universe, distinct, no doubt, but a part, a point of that immense network of forces and influences, physical and cosmic, vegetative and animal, ethnic, atavistic, hereditary, economic and historical, to whose laws we are subject. As we are individuals, we are subject to the stars. As we are persons, we rule them" (TR, 20-21).

For, if he is an *individual* in so far as he is a part of the universe, the human being is a *person* in so far as he is a spiritual subject. His personality finds its origin in the spirit.[12] "Spirit is the root of personality. The notion of personality thus involves that of totality and independence... To say that a

---

and part which Maritain wants to designate respectively by the terms person and individual" (p. 253). In "A Note on the Personalism of Jacques Maritain", *Philosophical Studies*, 1951, p. 37, M. Sadlier expresses the same view when he writes "the terminology would appear to be new", meaning new in relation to the terminology of Saint Thomas.

[10] "See with what religious pomp the modern world has proclaimed the sacred rights of the individual, and what a price it has paid for that proclamation. Yet was the individual ever more completely ruled by the great anonymous powers of the State, of Money, of Opinion? What then is the mystery? There is no mystery in it. It is simply that the modern world confounds two things which ancient wisdom has distinguished. It confounds individuality and personality" (TR, 19).

[11] "Not a personalist doctrine, but personalist aspirations confront us. There are, at least, a dozen personalist doctrines..." (*ibid.*, p. 12). "Our desire is to make clear the personalism rooted in the doctrine of St. Thomas and to separate, at the very outset, a social philosophy centred in the dignity of the human person from every social philosophy centred in the primacy of the individual and the private good. Thomistic personalism stresses the metaphysical distinction between individuality and personality" (*ibid.*, p. 13).

"This concept of man as at once an individual and a person lies, as I have indicated, at the heart of Maritain's practical philosophy." Charles FECHER, *The Philosophy of Jacques Maritain* (Westminster: The Newman Press, 1953), p. 156.

[12] "But, it is starting from the moment when immanent action appears in the world of life that spontaneity becomes a kind of, or rather a beginning of independence. However, independence only truly makes its entrance in the universe by a sudden break, when a being emerges endowed with interior freedom capable of determining for himself the ends of his action by his own intellectual activity (BT, 228), a being who by his choices 'becomes what he is'. Such is the personal subject, the person, an existent who controls and who possesses himself, a whole more than a part, 'a universe unto himself' whose autonomy is rooted in the intellect and who aims at achieving perfect independence; according to St. Thomas, the person 'is that which is noblest and highest in all nature' (EE, 11). There is the metaphysical foundation of Jacques Maritain's 'personalism'." Henry BARS, "Sujet et subjectivité selon Jacques Maritain", in *Les Etudes philosophiques*, January-March, 1975, 1, p. 42.

man is a person is to say that in the depth of his being he is more a whole than a part and more independent than servile'' (F, 214).

Because the human being is endowed with a trans-material intellect, the root of his freedom, he possesses a clear superiority over all other material beings. He is ''a centre inexhaustible, so to speak, of existence, bounty and action, capable of giving and of giving itself; capable of receiving not only this or that gift bestowed by another, but even another self as a gift, another self which bestows itself'' (PCG, 39). The human person as such, that is in so far as he is spirit, as interiority to itself, as capable of communicating with others in the order of knowledge and of love, is capable of self-possession, of self-perfecting and of free self-giving.

This distinction of the human being into individual and person should not be interpreted in a Manichean way for individuality in itself is good;[13] nor should it be interpreted in a dualistic way for the human being is both completely an individual and completely a person: ''There is not in me one reality, called my individual, and another reality, called my person. One and the same reality is, in a certain sense, an individual, and in another sense, a person. Our whole being is an individual by reason of that in us which derives from matter, and a person by reason of that in us which derives from spirit. Similarly, the whole of a painting is a physicochemical mixture by reason of the colouring stuff of which it is made, and the whole of it is a work of beauty by reason of the painter's art'' (PCG, 43). This is of capital importance and charged with consequences for education; Maritain insists: ''when you kill the individual, you also kill the person'' (C, 35).[14]

III.- THE HUMAN PERSON

Thus, the specific dignity of man stems from the fact that ''man is a person who holds himself in hand by his intelligence and his will'' (C, 7-8). Through his intellect, man can encompass the whole universe; the continuous progress of the sciences testify to it. Through his will, man is able to freely give himself in friendship and love (he can also hate). This confers upon the human person ''an absolute dignity because he is in direct relationship with the realm of being, truth, goodness, and beauty, and with God'' (C, 8).

Moreover this dignity is marked with the paradoxical seal of the human condition, its bipolarity. On one hand nothing is wasted like a human being; our civilization has surely increased the ''risks'' of human existence, but, at the same time, our civilization testifies to the tremendous effort employed to diminish — or at least to assume — the risks inherent in our carnal condition. Maritain expresses the paradox inherent in our condition in this way: ''but man is far from being a pure person; the human person is the person of a poor material individual, of an animal born more helpless than any other animal''

---

[13] ''Obviously as the very condition of our existence, it is something good. But it is precisely as related to personality that individuality is good. Evil arises when, in our action, we give preponderance to the individual aspect of our being'' (PCG, 43).
[14] We will come back to this important question in our third chapter.

(PCG, 60); still "he knows very well that death is not an end, but a beginning" (BT, 155).[15]

Respect for the person demands respect for his dignity; according to Maritain, this respect is even one of the basic criteria of a genuine civilization; it induces the best of us to be ready to give up their lives to defend the rights and freedom of the person.[16] A close reading of Maritain's writings reveals the lofty idea that he has of the human person: "no equivalent is to be found in the physical world" (RM, 3), and "nothing in the world is more precious than a single human being" (SH, 10).

And it is the spirit which is at the core of personality; the operations of the spirit as much in the noetic as in the affective order are the principal manifestations of personality.[17]

A. KNOWLEDGE OF THE TRUTH

Maritain's thought about the person presupposes a philosophy of knowledge whose importance is primary not only in the realm of ideas but also in the practical order. "If we are concerned with the future of civilization we must be concerned primarily with a genuine understanding of what knowledge is, its value, its degrees, and how it can foster the inner unity of the human being." (RR, 3).

Maritain has written many important books on knowledge: *Réflexions sur l'intelligence et sur sa vie propre* (1926), *The Degrees of Knowledge* (1932), *Science and Wisdom* (1935), *Quatre essais sur l'esprit dans sa condition charnelle* (1939), etc. In them he reveals the many sides of his philosophy of human knowledge and of his philosophy of the sciences. A thorough study of his theory of knowledge would go beyond the limitations of our subject. It seems to us that it would suffice to recall some of its most important aspects allowing one to better understand the human person and his education.

In order to get a good grasp on the scope of Maritain's theory of knowledge, first of all the basic distinction which exists between sensible and intellectual knowledge should be heeded.

Against empiricism which finds only a difference of degree between them, Maritain "maintains that there is a difference in nature between the senses and the intellect" (EM, 45). Still this difference should not be

---

[15] See on this topic Henry BARS, *Maritain en notre temps* (Paris: Grasset, 1959), pp. 261-265.

[16] "In each of us there dwells a mystery, and that mystery is the human personality. We know that an essential characteristic of any civilization worthy of the name is respect and feeling for the dignity of the human person. We know that in defence of the rights of the human person, just as in defence of liberty, we must be ready to give our lives" (RM, 2).

[17] "A person is a centre of liberty; a person confronts things, the universe, God; talks with another person, communicates with him by understanding and affection. The notion of personality, however complex it may be, belongs primarily to the ontological order. It is a metaphysical and substantial perfection which unfolds in the operative order in psychological and moral values" (DK, 231).

understood the way Kant does, according to which the spontaneity of the understanding is distinguished from the receptivity of sensibility. For Maritain — as for any Aristotelian or Thomistic philosopher — the senses and the intellect are powers of perception; the intellect has a proper object, an object which is perceived indeed depending on the senses, but an object which cannot be reduced to the sensible given. "The human mind, although being a reason handling its concepts and held to the strictest logic (it owes this to its carnal condition), is also an intellect, that is, a power capable of seeing in the intelligible order as the eye *sees* in the sensible order, but with incomparably more certitude. Is it not through such an intuition that the intellect knows the 'first principles' of every demonstration? (PG, 110). It is in this way that the human intellect can have "the intuition of being" (PG, 110) and that "knowledge is immersed in existence" (EE, 11).

This possibility that human reason has to be an understanding of being in the first place, even if by means of the chiaroscuro of sense knowledge, entails its primarily theoretical character; it is only by extension that it becomes practical. "For men are nourished by being; as their body lives by bread, their mind lives by being, by truth, by beauty; they have a measureless need of a constantly renewed impouring of these transcendentals. By the mere fact of applying itself to being, the intellect works for the good both of the City and of the universe. If we do not always grasp this, it is because we live most obviously in the senses and find a difficulty in representing to ourselves an activity which does not consist in producing something external, but which, being of an order superior to matter, remains and finds its completion in itself. Nevertheless, the immanent act of knowing — like the act of loving which depends upon it — has a life. Better it is life, life par excellence" (T, 11).

Human knowledge then has a life of its own in the activity by which it grasps what exists; it is not at first an *instrument* for the direction of human acts and the transformation of things — practical wisdom or art — it is first of all contemplation; and the modern world has a pressing need for contemplation. "The true solution would require that one succeed in strengthening these powers from within, in restoring the taste for truth within the minds of men, and in purifying and refreshing the sight of their eyes. Finally, in order to achieve these ends — and this is the point I want to make — there is only one remedy: to re-awaken in the world a sense of, and esteem for, contemplation. The world is prey to a great thirst, an immense mystical yearning which does not even know itself and which, because it remains without objective, turns to despair or neurosis" (RR, 48-49).[18]

The very life of the human intellect from its first intuitions up to the summit of its achievement — wisdom — is a constant search for the truth, which is its nourishment, and because of that "knowledge is a value in itself;

---

[18] "... the order of human values come to completion demands that practical action on the world and on the human community superabound from contemplation of truth, which means not only contemplation in its purest forms but, more generally, intellectual grasping of reality and enjoyment of knowledge for its own sake" (EM, 56).

and truth consists in the conformity of the mind with reality — with what is or exists independently of the mind. The intellect tends to grasp and conquer being. Its aim and its joy are essentially disinterested (EM, 47).[19]

The search for truth is natural for man; it is the essential sustenance of the mind. "Unless one loves the truth, one is not a man" (PG, 85). This doesn't mean that truth always yields itself to us in a spontaneous and complete way. Given the condition of an embodied spirit, all too often, the truth is attained — and only in a partial way — at the price of a laborious search subject to temporal laws. "It is essential for man to aspire to truth, and he has the capacity to reach it by his own powers — even if it can be in stumbling and zigzagging along the way, a way which is endless — in the things which depend on sense experience or to which such experience gives us indirect access" (PG, 95).

For the life of the mind is affected by the multiplicity inscribed in the heart of time; that is why the search for the truth finds expression in a multiplicity of noetic experiences which generate different kinds of knowledge: intuitive knowledge and discursive knowledge; common sense knowledge and logically structured knowledge; theoretical knowledge and practical knowledge; scientific, philosophical, artistic and mystical knowledge, and so forth.[20]

This multiplicity of knowledge, as a multiplicity, cannot satisfy the mind in its quest for universal knowledge, for wisdom, and in the search for unity. As the adage of the scholastic philosophers says *Ens, unum et verum convertuntur*. The meaning of truth implies that of unity. Distinguish in order to unite is the sub-title of *The Degrees of Knowledge*.[21] That is why "wisdom, which knows things eternal and creates order and unity in the mind, is superior to science or to knowledge through particular causes; and the theoretical intellect, which knows for the sake of knowing, comes before the practical intellect, which knows for the sake of action" (EM, 54). It is truth indeed which liberates the human person (EM, 48). But this liberation of the person through truth can only be achieved if knowledge tends toward unity in response to "the essential need and aspiration of the mind to be freed in unity" (C, 47).

From this point of view, Maritain adopts as his own the assertions of Aristotle relating to the importance of metaphysical wisdom as the higher expression of the development of the human intellect. "Thus, that superior kind of knowledge which is wisdom, because it deals not only with mastering natural phenomena but with penetrating the primary and most universal

---

[19] "The spontaneous response of common sense is that the truth is that which is, or rather, since it is the truth of knowledge which concerns us here, truth must obviously be found in the knowing mind; truth is the conformity of the mind with that which is" (RI, 11).

[20] See in this regard *The Degrees of Knowledge*.

[21] "A universal knowledge which is not unified and integrated according to a firmly recognized hierarchy of values is not universal knowledge but scattered and chaotic knowledge. Unity and integration are an essential need of natural intelligence." J. MARITAIN, *The Education of Man*, p. 97.

'raisons d'être' and with enjoying, as a final fruition, the spiritual delight of truth and the sapidity of being, fulfills the supreme aspiration of the intellectual nature and its thirst for liberation" (EM, 47). This wisdom is all the more important since "the dispersion and atomization of human life are in our day the great distress of the adult world" (C, 47).[22]

The necessity of a variety of ways of approaching the mystery of being, as an inevitable consequence of the condition of the human mind, and their rational character, that is as progressive knowledge based on the knowledge of sensible beings, implies as well the priority of the knowledge of external beings over that of the thinking and knowing subject and the imperfect quality of this self knowledge. Olivier Lacombe correctly expresses this important corollary of Maritain's philosophy. "If man's soul is not joined to a body from the outside, but in the ontological unity of a single substance, it completely informs an organized matter and is raised up to non-organic spiritual acts, it is normal that human knowledge be at first extroverted. It is no less true that by reflection on his acts — and also on those which proceed from him and he can recognize as his own — the human subject gains access to self-consciousness."[23]

Through this self-consciousness, the human being reaches a knowledge of the spiritual universe — the universe of interiority, of subjectivity — completely different from the knowledge of material things, though Maritain affirms their inexhaustible riches. He writes: "We shall never know everything there is to know about the tiniest blade of grass or the least ripple in a stream" (EE, 66-67). How much more mysterious and richer then will be that spiritual universe which is progressively disclosed to personal consciousness, the universe of the intellect, of love, of the person.

Thus Maritain is led to make a distinction within the domain of the human unconscious, a distinction of the first importance in the education process. "There are two kinds of unconscious, two great domains of psychological activity screened from the grasp of consciousness: the preconscious of the spirit in its living springs, and the unconsciousness of blood and flesh, instincts, tendencies, complexes, repressed images and desires, traumatic memories, as constituting a closed or autonomous dynamic whole. I would like to designate the first kind of unconscious by the name of spiritual or, for the sake of Plato, musical unconscious or preconscious; and the second by the name of automatic unconscious or deaf unconscious — deaf to the intellect, and structured into a world of its own apart from the intellect; we might also say, in quite a general sense, leaving aside any particular theory, Freudian unconscious" (CI, 91-92).

This distinction can afford us a better understanding of life in the concrete, for the two kinds of unconscious life, *spiritual* and *Freudian*, exert

---

[22] "Lastly, if it be true that the first thing necessary is to establish order within us, because every commencement is from within, the first condition of work for the establishment of a true order will be an entire subordination of the soul to truth" (FMW, 81).

[23] Olivier LACOMBE, "Jacques Maritain et la philosophie de l'être", in *Les Etudes philosophiques*, January-March, 1975, 1, p. 72.

their respective influences on our lives simultaneously and operate in a greater
or lesser way in the conscious activity with which they always "intermingle in
a greater or less degree" (CI, 92).

When it is a question in education whether to encourage the spontaneity
of the child, it should be remembered that spontaneity can mean either the
Freudian unconscious, the unconscious of the flesh, or the spiritual
unconscious, that of the "sources of knowledge and creativity, of love and
super-sensuous desires, hidden in the primordial translucid night of the
intimate vitality of the soul" (CI, 94).[24]

B. THE WILL, LOVE AND FREEDOM

This intimate vitality shares in the dynamism of being not only in the
order of knowledge, but also in the order of action. A philosophy of being is
at the same time a philosophy of the dynamism of being. In fact, according to
Thomistic philosophy, *ens, verum et bonum convertuntur,* which means that
being, that which is, is that which is true, and is nourishment for the mind;
being is also the good, that which attracts by its perfection, which fills by its
richness. "Now if being is superabundant and communicative of itself, if it
gives itself, love is thereby justified; justified also is that eros, that natural
love which is coextensive with being, and which instils in all things, at every
degree of being, an ineradicable and multiform propensity'" (EE, 43).[25]

And as a result, Maritain's philosophy, while remaining a philosophy of
the intellect, is at the same time a philosophy of the will, of love and of
freedom. If any form of being participates in its dynamism, the knowing
being, as such, is endowed with a corresponding dynamism which is called
the appetite; corresponding to sensible knowledge is a sensible appetite, and
corresponding to intellectual knowledge is the intellectual appetite whose
proper name is the will and whose principal act is love.[26]

"The intellect which abstracts and recognizes the objective form of
Being abstracts and recognizes also the objective form of Goodness — a thing
which is beyond the power of purely sensitive faculties. In every nature
endowed with intellect there ought therefore to be found a power of loving
and desiring essentially distinct from the sensitive appetite and tending to the
Good *as such,* to the Good in the universal and transcendental character in

---

[24]   In this regard, Maritain acknowledges the merits of Freud who refuses to identify
psychological facts with the facts of consciousness and who asserts the existence of an
unconscious composed of tendencies, desires and impulsions. On the other hand, he reproaches
Freud for seeing in the unconscious "the totality of the human being" and for neglecting the
higher functions. Maritain explains his position on Freud especially in "Freudianism and
Psychoanalysis", chapter 6 of *Scholasticism and Politics,* pp. 139-161.

[25]   "Now if being is superabundant and communicative of itself, if it gives itself, love is
thereby justified, and justified too that stimulation and that aspiration to emerge from self to share
the very life of the beloved which are consubstantial with the human being and which give
scandal to any philosophy of pure essence" (SH, 79).

[26]   "For the will is an appetite, it is characterized by desire, its primordial act is love; it is
not that imaginary and puritanical faculty which wills without desiring, claimed by Kant and
Thomas Reid" (BPT, 266).

which it comprehends each several good. This power we call the rational appetite or will" (FMW, 6-7). Consequently "the metaphysical mobility and the spirituality of the will come only from its being an appetite rooted in the intelligence" (TR, 44).

What is the proper object of the human will? As an intellectual appetite, the will has as its proper object the Good in itself, which means the Good capable of satisfying a human being, and bringing him felicity or happiness. The human will is of such a kind that it necessarily loves this Good, "so that we are not free not to will the good which saturates all desire (where it resides is another question) and we cannot voluntarily wiggle our finger without manifesting that we are made for beatitude, and that we necessarily will it" (BPT, 268).

And whereas this saturating being (God) cannot be grasped in all his richness in our carnal and earthy condition, we seek happiness without letup by a movement of transcending the imperfect beings which entreat us, never content and yet free, ever on the quest for a greater happiness. Thus the will only desires within the perspective of the good. "The will tends of necessity to something of which all it knows is that it satisfies all desire "and it is "free in face of every particular and partial good, of every good that we can take and measure and that is insufficient to exhaust the infinite capacity of the will to love" (FMW, 7).[27]

Therefore the human person can know being through his intellect, or better, he can know beings according to their analogical richness, starting from the most imperfect beings and ascending to personal beings, and right on up to God; because he is endowed with a free will, he can also love the good in its analogical diversity, and more particularly love other persons with the love of friendship, seeking in and through love his perfection and his happiness. "When we say that the perfection of human life consists in love, we mean that this perfection consists in a relationship and in communication between persons, and primarily between the person of man and that of God (SH, 83).[28]

The human person is endowed with an intellect which allows him to receive being, and with a will by which he can freely give himself to other beings. These two complementary expressions of the human spirit, each

---

[27] In "The Conquest of Freedom", Maritain presents the same idea in a more precise and more explicit way. "Spirit as such implies a sort of infinity; its faculty of desire of itself seeks a good which satisfies absolutely, therefore a good without limit, and we cannot have any desire which is not comprehended in this general desire for happiness. But as soon as reflection occurs, our intelligence, confronted with goods that are not the Good, and judging them so, brings into actuality the radical determination that our appetite for happiness possesses in regard to everything which is not happiness itself. Efficacious motivation of an intelligent being can be only a practical judgment; and this judgment owes to the will the whole of its efficaciousness; it is will, impelled by its own unpredicatble initiative towards the good presented to it by such and such a judgment, that gives this judgment the power of specifying the will efficaciously" (F, 213).

[28] Maritain has explained his conception of love and of friendship in *Carnet de notes* (1965), pages 302-354 and in *Approches sans entraves* (1973), pp. 202-339.

having its own value and each its own meaning, respectively make manifest the mystery of the person. As did his master Saint Thomas, Maritain "shows us two complementary but essentially different activities in every spirit, each as exacting and voracious as the other: an activity wholly turned towards the being of the object, towards what is 'other' as it is 'other', and of itself only concerned with that, living only for it — the intelligence; and an activity wholly occupied with the good of the subject or of the things with which the subject is united, which itself is concerned only with the good, living only for it — the will. Each is predominant in its order, the one absolutely and for knowledge, the other relatively and for action. Woe to humanity if one monopolizes all the nourishment at the expense of the other" (TR, 41-42).[29]

This teaching about the distinction between and the complementarity of the life of the intellect and the dynamism of the will is of capital importance if one is to understand Maritain's philosophy of education. It is in the name of this teaching, in *Education at the Crossroads* (C, 18-22),[30] that he is as strongly opposed to intellectualism as he is to voluntarism, both of which are one-sided and extreme views of the powers of the human soul, both views which education must guard against.

Following Maritain, it is evident that the person is a communicating being and a communal being. The human person can only fulfil himself according to his innate capacities by communicating with other beings through knowledge and in community with them through love. In this way the philosophy of being becomes a philosophy of the spirit and a philosophy of subjectivity. The intuition of being already reveals in an implicit way what the metaphysics of the person allows to be made explicit. In *The Range of Reason,* Maritain points this out in a magnificent way: "For when the intuition of Being and Existence takes place in me, it normally carries along with itself another intuition of my own existence or myself, the intuition of subjectivity as subjectivity. Now subjectivity, insofar as it is subjectivity, is not an object presented to thought, but rather the very wellspring of thought — a deep, unknown and living centre which superabounds in knowledge and superabounds in love, attaining only through love its supreme level of existence, existence as giving itself" (RR, 91).[31]

---

[29]   "There is a mistake to be avoided on the intellectualism of St. Thomas. He proclaims unceasingly the superiority of the intellect over the will, considered according to the absolute hierarchy of the faculties: and he maintains the pure sovereignty of the intellect in the order of speculative knowledge. But, on the other hand, he maintains, that it is by the will that man is good or bad, using the words 'good' and 'bad' absolutely and without qualification: he makes judgment depend, in the order of practical and prudential activity, on the appetitive faculties — the faculties, that is of the will and upon their rectification: and above all, he most definitely affirms the pre-eminence, considered according to the conditions of this world, of love in human life" (T, 37).

[30]   This question will be examined in Chapter Three.

[31]   In pages 91 and 92 which should be quoted at length, Maritain shows how the intuition of being is accompanied by "the discovery of the actual abyss of subjectivity. At the same time, it is the discovery of the basic generosity of existence" (RR, 91).

IV.- THE PERSON AND SOCIETY

By virtue of his basic dynamism, the human person is a communal being and, as a result, he yearns to live in society. "The person is a whole. It is not a little god without doors or windows, like Leibnitz's monad, or an idol which sees not, hears not, speaks not. It tends by its very nature to social life and communion" (RM, 5). This natural aspiration to the social life is a response both to the needs and the perfections of the person.

It is quite clear that this being, born "the least provided for of all animals", has need of a social life to assure his survival and his development. Society is necessary for him in supplying his material needs (food, clothing, shelter, etc.) and also to provide for his more specific needs which are education and the aid of his fellow men, requisites for the achievement of human dignity. "Society appears, therefore, to provide the human person with just those conditions of existence and development which it needs" (PCG, 34).

Therefore the congenital indigence of human beings makes society a requirement. But the opulence of the person seeks as well to find expression in a communal and social life; the person is a communal being, an opening to communications of knowledge and of love. "In its radical generosity, the human person tends to overflow into social communications in response to the law of superabundance inscribed in the depths of being, life, intelligence and love" (PCG, 34).

The vital and necessary insertion of man in society does not occur without raising the most complex problems of social philosophy and of the philosophy of education, namely, the problem of the relations between the person and society, the problem of the relations between the individual and personal good and the common good. This problem of relations "gives rise to the conflict of individualism and personality".[32]

Maritain's position on this issue follows a middle road. As he rejects the individualism which would completely subordinate the common good to individual freedoms, so too he rejects any form of statism or of collectivism which would sacrifice the human person to social imperatives. The metaphysical distinction between individuality and personality allows us to consider the human being as at once a part of the commonwealth (insofar as he is an individual) and as a whole, transcending the imperatives of the social organization (insofar as he is a person). "It is because he is first an individual of a species that man, having need of the help of his fellows to perfect his specific activity, is consequently an *individual* of the city, a member of society. And on this count he is subordinated to the good of his city as to the good of the whole, the common good which as such is more

[32] J. MARITAIN, "Le thomisme et la civilisation", *Revue de philosophie*, 1928, p. 120. The well known controversy which was raised between Charles de Konninck and Jacques Maritain about the primacy of the common good or the primacy of the personal good led Maritain to present a synthesis of his positions on this question in *The Person and the Common Good* in 1947.

divine and therefore better deserving the love of each than his very own life. But if it is a question of the destiny which belongs to man as a *person*, the relation is inverse, and it is the human city which is subordinate to his destiny'' (TR, 22).[33]

In fact, to the extent that he is an individual, the human being enters into society with his fellow men as a part whose particular good is, as such, inferior to the good of the social whole. The good life shared in common requires that the human individual be subordinated to the just laws of the commonwealth, and it requires an active participation in society, and an assumption of one's social responsibilities, and so forth. Ultimately this participation may lead to giving up one's life for the defence of the values of civilization whose depository is the life of the community and whose defender is the polity.

But the good of the social whole is only truly a common good, if it is distributed to the persons of the society, respecting their dignity. In this sense the common good is subordinated to the good of the persons involved. ''It includes within itself as principal value, the highest access, compatible with the good life of the whole, of the persons to their life of person and liberty of expansion, as well as to the communication of generosity consequent upon such expansion'' (PCG, 51).[34]

The mystery of the person transcends the society, the state, and the common good, and the common good of the city is ordered to the good of the person, to the conquest of his perfection and of his spiritual freedom which belong to an order higher than that of the city. ''The universe of truth — truths of science, of wisdom and of poetry — to which the intellect tends of itself, belongs by nature to a higher sphere than the political community. There are things in the natural order as in the supernatural order that the state cannot touch: the secrets of the heart constitute the free act as such, the universe of moral laws and the right of the conscience to hearten to God and make its way toward him'' (SH, 62-63).

The kind of social and political organization that Maritain proposes results quite naturally from this comprehension of the dynamic relations existing between the person and the common good. An individualistic society tends to deny ''that man, by reason of certain things which are in him, is engaged in his entirety as a part of political society'' (PCG, 72). A denial which dissolves the reality of the common good as such. On the other hand, a totalitarian or ''communist'' society tends to consider human individuals as only parts of a social whole and thus dissolves the mystery of the person. A society of human persons, a society of free men can only be a society which is both personalist and communalist, a society in which ''to feel responsible for one's brothers does not lessen freedom though it puts on it a heavier load'' (IH, 183). For ''the relation of the individual to society must be conceived after an irreducibly human and specifically ethico-social pattern, that is,

---

[33] See also PCG, 47-59.
[34] See also RM, 9 and TH, 121-123.

personalist and communalist at the same time; the organization to be accomplished is one of liberties. But an organization of liberties is unthinkable apart from the moral realities of justice and civil amity, which, on the natural and temporal plane, correspond to what the Gospel calls brotherly love on the spiritual and supernatural plane'' (PCG, 102).[35]

Understood in this way, political society is not just a powerful lever of economic progress whose primary objective would be to increase the GNP (the gross national product, that divinity of our industrial society) or the material affluence of its citizens. Through a dialectic of reciprocal overlapping of individual and social values, of personal and communal values, the commonwealth behaves as a civilizing force, as a promoter of what is human. "For this philosophy the political task is par excellence a task of civilization and culture; it tends above all to provide the common good of the multitude in such a way that the concrete person, not only within the category of the privileged, but in the whole mass, truly accedes to the measure of independence which is compatible with civilized life and which is assured alike by the economic guarantees of labor and property, political rights, civic virtues and the cultivation of the mind'' (CD, 68).

Thus there is no antinomy between the dignity of the human person and the society, quite the contrary. Man's offspring cannot see the light of day and grow unless the gift of life is given to him, unless the commonwealth (that is, the family, the state...) make him welcome and allow him to develop his personal being which, by reason of his natural condition, he only possesses in a germinal way, but which he can progressively construct and conquer, as a communal being, as a free being. It is this which makes possible both the progress of persons and that of societies. "To return to more strictly political considerations, we must note that the roots of this movement of progression lie the natural aspirations of the human person to his freedom of expansion and autonomy and towards a political and social emancipation which will release him more and more from the bonds of material nature. The movement under discussion, then, leads, within social life itself, to the progressive realization of man's longing to be treated as a person, that is to say, as a whole'' (RM, 34).

In order to better understand this progress of the person and his liberation in and through social history, it is easy to see that we must clarify this reality of human freedom which is at the core of the mystery of the person and without which, communion and gift, love and friendship become meaningless words; and without this reality of human freedom the twofold character of the commonwealth as personalist and communalist becomes fool's gold, an illusion.

---

[35] "Society is a whole whose parts are themselves wholes, and it is an organism composed of liberties, not just of vegetative cells" (RM, 8).

Chapter II

Freedom and the Freedoms

I.- A PHILOSOPHY OF FREEDOM

"A person is a universe of spiritual nature endowed with freedom of choice and constituting to this extent a whole which is independent in face of the world, neither nature nor the state can lay prey to this universe without its permission. And God himself, who is and acts within, acts there in a particular manner and with a particularly exquisite delicacy, which shows the value He sets on it: He respects its freedom, at the heart of which He nevertheless lives; He solicits it, He never forces it" (IH, 9).

This means that the mystery of the person is also a mystery of freedom, to such an extent that bereft of this freedom, the person would vanish as a person; if fraternal friendship or the love of God were imposed on us, would they still be friendship and love? A human community without freedom would resemble more the army of robot-men so well described in Aldous Huxley's *Brave New World*[1] than a society of human persons. Everything might function wonderfully there, but nothing in it would be human.

It is why the personalist philosophy of Maritain, as that of Saint Thomas from which it draws its inspiration, is and has to be a philosophy of freedom. "The philosophy of Saint Thomas is not only a philosophy of Nature or, more generally, of Being, but it is also, and particularly from the angle of Ethics, a Philosophy of Freedom: as, from the angle of Knowledge, it is a Philosophy of Mind or Spirit; a philosophy too of Freedom and a Philosophy of Mind or Spirit that connects one with another to a point of ultimate convergence. But in place of opposing the order of Freedom to the order of Nature or of Being, the philosophy of St. Thomas unites without confusing them, and grounds the former on the latter." (FMW, 4)

---

[1] Aldous HUXLEY, *Brave New World* (New York: Harper and Row, 1946). "Standard men and women; in uniform batches. The whole of a small factory staffed with the products of a single bokanovskified egg.
    'Ninety-six identical twins working ninety-six identical machines!' The voice was almost tremulous with enthusiasm. 'You really know where you are. For the first time in history.' He quoted the planetary motto. 'Community, Identity, Stability.' Grand words. 'If we could bokanovskify indefinitely the whole problem would be solved' " (*ibid.*, p. 6).

It is important to clarify the relation which exists between nature and freedom; in this respect, Maritain refuses to reduce freedom to a spiritual spontaneity or to a natural determinism according to which man would only be a "multitude of connections in the phenomenal order" (FMW, 3); he rejects as well a freedom which would be completely cut off from the natural order, especially the Kantian disjunction between nature and freedom.

According to the Maritainian conception of freedom, the world of freedom originates in nature, but it is distinct from nature and "constitutes a world apart", the world of culture; this culture, a product of reason and freedom, extends the world of nature of which it is the natural fulfillment: "Culture answers the fundamental aspiration of human nature, but it is the world of the spirit and liberty adding their efforts to the effort of nature" (RC, 4).[2]

The human individual receives at birth a nature, but he receives it in an incomplete and imperfect state. This nature will grow and will develop, of course, according to definite natural laws, passing through childhood, youth and maturity, and finally, death; but the spirit which dwells in this nature makes of it a free being capable, with the help of other men, of taking up the gifts of nature, of perfecting them and of giving them a meaning and a completion.[3] "And man, as part of nature, has an essence which is good in itself. We see that the evolution of the cosmos is a persevering, though constantly thwarted, movement toward higher forms of life and consciousness, which achieves a final victory in the human species and is taken over, within the limits of the latter, by human liberty" (RR, 201).[4]

In a certain sense, this freedom makes us into gods. Of course, it is not a question of that gratuitous and baseless freedom of Sartrian existentialism, a freedom which has no meaning outside of itself and which, in its absolute as well as absurd character, implies the denial of God;[5] rather it is a question of a freedom which is a divine gift and bears God's mark on it,[6] but this freedom is also marked with the seal of our weakness. There is "in human freedom a participated similitude of divine freedom, thanks to which, without being able to create anything properly speaking *(ex nihilo)*, we, however, as we please, cause that to be which was not and also form ourselves; thanks to which we are persons and, like gods, intervene in the order of the world by acts of

---

[2]   "The truly and fully natural man is not nature's man, the uncultivated soil, but the virtuous man, the human soil cultivated by undeviating reason, man formed by the inner culture of the intellectual and moral virtues. He alone has a consistency, a personality" (RC, 7).

[3]   "But we men, merely because we know the sense of the word Being and of the word Why, and because into our poor head the whole heavens (and more than the heavens) can be fitted, we are lost before we take our first step. We must lay out the road we follow; we must deliberate our end" (FMW, 14-15).

[4]   "The individual's entire life is nothing but a process of giving birth to himself; in truth we are only fully born when we die." E. FROMM, *Le drame fondamental de l'homme: naître à l'humain*, quoted by Edgar FAURE and others *Learning to Be*, p. 158.

[5]   See Jean-Paul SARTRE, *Existentialism and Humanism* (London: Metheun, 1970). "Man is nothing else but that which he makes of himself" *(ibid.,* p. 28).

[6]   See DESCARTES, *Meditation IV.*

endless scope; so much so that the mystery of our *activity* is as marvelous and as terrifying for whoever can be conscious of it, as the very mystery of our being'' (BPT, 274).

By our freedom, then, we can assert ourselves as persons, we can build, at least partially, our personal reality. "The free act is not only the act of the person as such, it is moreover, — and this is perhaps the same thing, — the revelation of the person to itself'' (SP, 127).[7]

In order to better understand, and to appreciate at its true worth, the position of Maritain in regard to the mystery of human freedom, and the dynamics of education (which is an education for freedom), it is essential to set down precisely the different meanings of the word freedom in his philosophy, for "the word *freedom,* — like all big words for which men are ready to die, and which are laden, not only with the riches of the object, but with the desires, the dreams and the supreme generosities of the subject, — the word freedom conveys a great number of meanings; and yet these meanings, though widely different, have something in common'' (SP, 117).

Maritain's thinking on freedom includes two principal lines of significa- tion. There is freedom as absence of constraint, that is, freedom of spontaneity, naturally enjoyed by every human being who can act in accordance with its nature, without any outside factor coming to thwart the expression of action as the law of being: *Agere sequitur esse.* In the human being this freedom is given in an initial and incipient state, and because within this freedom — and as its specific extension — another freedom is situated (the freedom of choice), it can conquer an even greater spontaneity which develops into the freedom of autonomy, the freedom of perfection. Over and above this freedom, conceived as the absence of external constraint, the person enjoys freedom as the *absence of inner necessity,* freedom as active self-determination, freedom of choice. "An act of free will is an act that no necessity, be it completely internal and exempt from any external pressure, determines'' (BT, 189).

Maritain's philosophy of freedom implies then, from its starting point, a distinction between the freedom of spontaneity and the freedom of choice (or free will), and a distinction between the different degrees of the freedom of spontaneity, beginning with the initial — and minimal — spontaneity given at birth and as far as the terminal freedom — "the freedom of perfection and exultation'' which can be conquered by a judicious exercise of free will and by the help of appropriate social arrangements. This progressive conquest of

---

[7]   "Man, the human subject is but a 'person in embryo' (SP, 131). If it is right to see in the free act 'not only the act of the person as such, it is moreover, — and this is perhaps the same thing, — the revelation of the person to itself' (SP, 127), it should be added that 'one knows real personality and real liberty, while the other does not' (SP, 132). For what is given in the structure of the spiritual subject is the metaphysical root of personality, but in the order of action, by which 'I become what I am', I must win and pay dearly for my personality as for my freedom (SP, 131)." Henry BARS, "Sujet et subjectivité selon Jacques Maritain", in *Les Etudes philosophiques*, January-March, 1975, 1, p. 43.

the freedom of perfection as much in social conditions as in personal lives constitutes what Maritain calls *the dynamism of freedom*.[8]

II.- THE FREEDOM OF SPONTANEITY

If the freedom of spontaneity is conceived as the absence of outer constraint and belongs to every being which acts in accordance with its nature,[9] it follows that there is a freedom of spontaneity proper to each degree of being and that, consequently, the freedom of spontaneity admits of degrees. In the kingdom of worldly beings, of which human nature is the peak, Maritain distinguishes four degrees of the freedom of spontaneity.

At the bottom of the scale, there is the spontaneity of material nature in general, "limited exclusively to the transitive activity mutually exercised and received" and which belongs to every material being, to every *natural being*. "Nature", according to Aristotle, "is a source or cause of being moved and of being at rest in that to which it belongs primarily, in virtue of itself and not in virtue of a concomitant attribute".[10] Thus, a stone falls "freely" (or in a free fall), the planets move themselves spontaneously, according to the laws of nature, etc. It is important to note that natural spontaneity requires, as a condition of its exercise, the action of surrounding bodies, which action, far from exerting any violence on the natural and the spontaneous movement, makes it possible; and so it is at every level of spontaneity, with the exception of divine freedom. That is why no created freedom enjoys or can enjoy a total and absolute independence.

The organisms which live a vegetative existence possess a second degree of spontaneity which expresses itself in the immanent character of their proper activity; in accordance with its constituted structure, the plant lives, that is, assimilates the nutrients drawn from the soil, transforms them into its substance, grows, produces germinating cells capable of reproducing other vegetative organisms. Through its immanent activity — an activity constituted by the transitive activities of one part of the organism on another part — the plant is freer than the stone; it has a greater spontaneity, one qualitatively higher than that of a non-living thing.

---

[8] "With Maritain, the philosophy of freedom is completely encased in the distinction commonly accepted by Scholastic philosophers between the *freedom of spontaneity*, which excludes constraint, and the *freedom of choice*, which excludes necessity. In reality, the former is divided in two. There is a spontaneity inseparable from the will as such, which, by definition, cannot be forced to act (for to be forced to act is to act against one's will). Moreover this spontaneity is found also proportionately in whatever is living, and even in whatever *acts*, in the full sense of the term; and Maritain describes the degrees of spontaneity in a fine study to which we shall return. But besides this generic and rudimentary spontaneity, there is a terminal spontaneity, the triumphant affirmation of the being at last changed intrinsically, that 'freedom of autonomy and exultation' which holds such a high place, with Maritain, as we shall see. Between the two, relying on the first and tending toward the second, is freedom in the most common meaning of the word, the freedom of choice." Joseph DE FINANCE, "La philosophie de la liberté chez Maritain," in *Recherches et Débats*, (19), 1957, pp. 95-96.

[9] "It does not imply the absence of necessity but merely the absence of constraint. It is the power of acting by virtue of its own internal inclination and without undergoing the coaction imposed by an exterior agent" (F, p. 215).

[10] *Physics* II, c. 1, 192b 21-22.

The sensitive life comprises a third degree of spontaneity which is distinguished from the two preceding ones in a rather special way. In fact the two preceding ones have a spontaneous activity which corresponds to the natural form of their physical being; moreover, the animal enjoys a new kind of spontaneity based on the immanence of sense knowledge; it moves itself according to a form which it has acquired through knowledge: the internal and external senses and instinct become "inner" principles of action and of expression. Thus the bird flies freely and sings by means of forms which are psychic structures, it moves itself spontaneously by means of acquired "intentional" forms.

Man, endowed with intelligence, is found at a fourth degree of spontaneity, that of the life of the mind by which he acquires a superior spontaneity, the freedom of autonomy; he can act according to ends which are self-imposed. "Being capable of going beyond the moment of sensation, and to know being and the intelligible natures, he knows what he does, and he knows the end of his acts as such; by his own intellectual activity, he determines for himself the ends of his action" (BT, 228).

The life of the mind allows the human being to achieve the independence of a person at once intelligent and endowed with free will; this zone of independence is the zone of human creativity. It includes a minimal freedom, that of the initial spontaneity of our spiritual powers, the intellect and the will, and free choice is rooted in it (which we shall discuss in the following paragraph). But the life of the mind contains a hope as well, a vocation whose realization is made possible by the good use of free will, the vocation for a superior autonomy, to a maximal or terminal freedom. This freedom which Maritain calls the freedom of expansion or the freedom of perfection, the freedom of independence or of exultation, "does not consist merely in following the inclination of nature but in being or making oneself actively the sufficient principle of one's own operation; in other words, in perfecting oneself as an indivisible whole in the act one brings about. This is why freedom of independence exists only in beings which also have free will, and presupposes the exercise of free will in order to arrive at its end" (F, 215).

In other words, the "vital space" which is located between the initial freedom and the terminal freedom is all that space occupied by the life of the mind, animated by the radical love of the saturating good, and impelling the person to seek this good: "the most fundamental aspiration of the person is the aspiration towards the liberty of expansion and autonomy" (RM, 44). It is the revelation of the person to himself.[11] The true freedom of autonomy of persons is at one with spiritual perfection (IH, 134), and the freedom of choice is the means of conquering it.

---

[11] "I have already cited St. Thomas's aphorism, that the whole root of liberty is established in the reason. What reveals subjectivity to itself is not an irrational break (however profound and gratuitous it may be) in an irrational flow of moral and psychological phenomena, of dreams, automatisms, urges and images surging upwards from the unsconcious. Neither is it the anguish of forced choice. It is self-mastery for the purpose of self-giving" (EE, 82).

At the top of the degrees of spontaneity the incommensurable spontaneity of God is found, the absolute spontaneity which, in its perfection, is the primary source of all spontaneity and all perfection, an indescribable spontaneity and freedom whose riches we can only express in the stammering of our analogical knowledge and whose mystery is set forth in revelation.

III.- THE FREEDOM OF CHOICE

Freedom of choice, or free will, is, according to Maritain, the very root of the world of personal freedom. Undoubtably it is given to us, but its role is determinative in the process of personalization; it is by the freedom of choice that the person can conquer his freedom of autonomy, that we can become "persons having dominion over our own acts" (FMW, 30). In fact, it is by free will that our acts are properly human; only free acts — those emanating from free choice — are morally good or bad, and imputable to the person, and through the exercise of this freedom we can attain to the fulfillment of our personal being. Thus, it is understandable why "all the varied senses of the word Freedom which have importance for mankind presuppose this primordial freedom, this fact that our will and its inner fortress is free not only from all external constraint but also from any kind of inherent necessity that would determine it *ad unum*" (FMW, 5).

A. THE EXISTENCE OF THE FREE WILL

A basic question then arises, a question of crucial importance for the philosophy of education: do we really enjoy a freedom which "is not the absurd power of choosing without motive or in spite of motive, but the power of choosing according to reason" (BPT, 275)?

According to absolute intellectualism, free will doesn't exist in us; the intellect cannot be influenced by a will which always "chooses" what the intellect judges to be the best. This metaphysical position is found in one way or another in the great metaphysicians of the classical period, especially in Spinoza according to whom the impossibility of the free will is a result of the fact that "there is nothing contingent given in nature, but everything in it is determined by the necessity of the divine nature to exist and to produce some effect in a certain way".[12]

Pure empiricists likewise deny the existence of free will: "to the extent that science reveals dynamic elements working in our psychical activity, they see in the mere existence of these elements the proof that the same operate in a necessarily determining fashion — which is precisely what remains to be proved" (F, 211).

---

[12]   See *Ethics*, I, prop. XXIX and XLVIII.
"Let us state then that there is no free will in the human soul. Nothing in the world can be independent of God, and the course of events which results necessarily and according to eternal laws cannot depend on the capriciousness of the individual. Man believes that he is free, because being conscious of his actions, he is ignorant of their causes; but we know very well that every action has a cause... "ALAIN, *Spinoza* (Paris: Gallimard, Idées, 1949), p. 81.

For instance, Hume, discussing the regularity and constancy that can be observed in human actions, concludes from it that the connection which exists between motives and voluntary actions is similar to that which exists between natural causes and natural effects; as a consequence, he asserts that "there is only a kind of necessity as there is only a kind of cause and that the current distinction between moral and physical necessity is without foundation in nature".[13] The freedom that we like to pride ourselves in would be then but a name that we give to the necessities governing human action.

Contrary to both absolute intellectualism and empiricism, Maritain asserts — moreover without any hesitation — the existence of the freedom of choice: "it is", he writes, "the most certain fact there is" (BPT, 252); each of us knows, by the first natural operation of the spontaneous consciousness, that we enjoy the freedom of choice. We know very well, for example, "that if we betray a friend, risk our property to aid some unfortunate, decide to become a banker, monk or soldier, these kinds of acts are what they are only because we have involved therein our personality and have arranged that they be so rather than not" (F, 210).[14]

It concerns then a fact of experience whose evidence is prior to any philosophical reflection and which no philosophy can legitimately challenge. Here, Maritain goes along with Descartes following whom "we are so assured of freedom and of the indifference which is in us, that there is nothing that we know more clearly".[15] Besides, the judgments of practical reason, the principles of social life, the universal agreement of men bear witness to the fact of the freedom of choice which is "an immediate datum of consciousness; it is perceived by an intuition as infallible as the intuition of the active self by the consciousness, or of the external world by the senses, or of being by intelligence" (BPT, 252).

B. The Nature of Free Will

However, if "each of us knows very well *that* he possesses freedom of choice" (F, 210), "each of us knows very poorly *wherein* freedom of choice lies." (F, 210) The philosophical elucidation of what free will is and the

---

[13]   *Treatise of Human Nature* (New York: Dutton, Evereyman's Library, 1956), Vol. I, p. 168.
    "Next when science becomes for man a conception of life which encompasses everything (scientism), then it will definitely try to remove any space for freedom. The explicable will be considered as what is not yet explained. And then we shall only believe ourselves to be free insofar as we are ignorant of the necessity and determination which surrounds us on all sides. The so-called consciousness of freedom is nothing other than the ignorance of causes." Francesco VIOLA, "La liberté humaine entre liberté absolue et déterminisme", in *Nova et Vetera,* 1976, p. 118.
[14]   "Because we are spirits by what is best in us, we can have experience of things of the spirit even while we still remain on the level of nature. It is thus that we know experimentally not only the existence of our soul and of our free choice, but that we can also attain a certain obscure experimental perception of the very freedom of the spirit within us and its transcendence in respect to the whole material universe, or even (as many documents of contemporary literature attest) of the nothingness immanent to all created things" (DK, 278-279).
[15]   DESCARTES, *Principles* I, 41.

analysis of its foundations can be of considerable use here, so "the way in which St. Thomas discovers for us *the nature* of free will is at the same time the proof that free will exists necessarily in every intelligent nature" (BT, 191).[16]

Maritain conceives the world of freedom as an extension of the world of nature in which it is grounded and which it presupposes; this conception of the relations of nature and freedom is verified in regard to free will. In fact "in the teaching of St. Thomas" — and in that of Maritain — "freedom of choice is not an irrational element thrust on the philosopher by the moral consciousness; it is a thing proper to a certain nature, in short, to the rational or intellectual nature. St. Thomas writes 'the whole root of freedom lies in reason'. To be free is of the essence of every intellectual being" (FMW, 5-6). Since the root of the freedom of choice is in the intellect or reason, it then becomes possible to understand that the human being can establish its existence. "I am taking it for granted that we also admit that man is a being gifted with intelligence, and who, as such, acts with an understanding of what he is doing, and therefore with the power to determine for himself the ends which he pursues" (MS, 78). Therefore it is important to have a good grasp on the connection which exists between the intelligent character of our action and freedom.

By our will, we proceed toward the good things known by the intellect *sub ratione boni.*[17] But, the will, *ut natura,* that is, by virtue of its own nature, wills or loves necessarily and spontaneously the good which satiates, beatitude; that which is not the satiating good — absolute and universal — cannot necessitate the will which becomes, by extension, undetermined relative to any particular or partial good and to any good perceived as particular or partial. This indetermination or this indifference cannot be removed except by an active self-determination of the will, by the free choice of a particular good and even of the concrete good of the person.[18] This free choice results from a fruitful interaction between the intellect and the will; in a reciprocal causality exercised at the heart of the deliberation which terminates in choice, the specification of the will by the intellect itself depends on the exercise of the will. The mystery of this dependence is located in the mastery of the will over the practical judgment which itself determines the will. It concerns then an act of the person precisely as person. I necessarily will happiness; now the act about which the intellect deliberates is a particular good which lacks the power to fill to satisfaction, which does not constitute happiness; then "the will brings the intellect to pass...to a practically-

---

[16] "Not only therefore do we experience within us the fact of freedom, through our awareness that the act which emanates from our deliberate will is so dependent on us to be ours to the very essence of its being and even to the reason which elicits it; but it is also possible (for the Thomist) to show that an intellectual being is of necessity endowed with freedom" (FMW, 6).

[17] See Chapter I, pages.

[18] "St. Thomas deduces freedom (here) from necessity (there). Because the will is *internally* and *naturally necessitated* to absolutely satisfying happiness, it is free with regard to everything else; that is to say, with respect to everything it can desire here on earth, — for where on earth is this perfect happiness, this complete satiety of desire?" (SP, 120).

practical judgment, which alone is capable of determining the act efficaciously" (SP, 124).

It should be remembered that in Maritain's teaching, the human intellect, by reason of its concrete condition as an embodied spirit, is abstractive and can only present to the will abstract ideas — Spinoza would say inadequate knowledge; — consequently, every concrete good, even God the most perfect, is the object of an election, of a free choice, of a love that it must choose.[19] Another consequence of this fact is, to the extent that the life of the mind is active, in which man acts as in a conscious and deliberate way, the passions are unable, by themselves, to determine a *human* action, even if the passions have a more or less strong power of attraction over it. "The reply to the determinists here, which Bergson does not afford, is that motives (in the strict sense of the word) can in no way be compared to more or less great forces acting upon us because they are not inclinations and motives, but ideas or judgments of the intelligence" (BPT, 256).[20]

It is for this reason that denying the intellect denies freedom; the free will results from our nature as intelligent beings. "To be free is to be master of one's judgment, *liberii arbitrii*. The will is able to control the judgment which determines its act and by virtue of this control, it has complete mastery of its action" (FMW, 10).

On the other hand, the free act is not reduced to the order of thought; it is situated in the order of affectivity, in an activity which is rooted in the intellect and which cannot be exercised without its concurrence, but which involves the will, this *facultas suppositi,* and, consequently actively involves the whole person in the action which flows from it. "There is here, in the last analysis, a primacy of exercise over specification which shocks every philosophy of pure essence and which has meaning only because at the indivisible instant when will and intellect determine each other, the act of the will causes the subject to exist, decidedly, according to the particular attitude or disposition of its whole moral nature, in relation to which a particular good will be appropriate to that subject; and that same act of the will renders the

---

[19] The creature "can be endowed with the freedom of choice only if it possesses a fallible freedom, that is, if it can converse with God, not only obeying the flux of divine actions and motions, but also by resisting them, by saying No, impeding in itself the action of God" (SP, 137-138).

"Nonetheless the root of freedom is reason itself. Only the unlimited scope of the intellect opened to the infinity of Being and beings, and the unlimited aspiration of the will and love for the infinity of the Good make possible a free choice between the finite goods which entreat us, none of which is identical with infinite goodness." O. LACOMBE, "Jacques Maritain et la philosophie de l'être", in *Les Etudes philosophiques,* January-March, 1975, 1, pp. 76-77.

[20] "In general, human free will does not exclude but presupposes the vast and complex dynamism of instincts, tendencies, psychophysical dispositions, acquired habits, and hereditary traits, and it is at the top point where this dynamism emerges in the world of spirit that freedom of choice is exercised, to give or withhold decisive efficacy to the inclinations and urges of nature. It follows from this that freedom, as well as responsibility, is capable of a multiplicity of degrees of which the author of being alone if judge. It does not follow from this that freedom does not exist — on the contrary! If it admits of degrees, then it exists" (F, 212).

corresponding judgment of the intellect efficacious, or, in other words, causes it to get a grip on existence decidedly'' (EE, 40-41).

This mutual overlapping of the intellect and the will, that is, of the two poles — the noetic pole and the affective pole — of the person as person in the dynamics of eliciting the free act is fraught with consequences for education, and thereafter it is understandable, if such indeed is the way that things happen in the mystery of freedom, why Maritain is opposed both to intellectualism and to voluntarism in education.[21]

The Maritainian conception of the freedom of choice has important metaphysical and moral implications. Like the intellect in which it takes root, the free will reveals the spirituality inherent in human nature as well as its accession to values and moral responsibility.[22]

Another corollary of the freedom of our action is the contingent character of human acts insofar as they originate in freedom. The occurrence of freedom is not determined by its antecedents — to the considerable shock of those who hold to a universal determinism and who prefer to sacrifice the fact of freedom to their theory —; there is not in the free act as such any factual necessity as in matters of chance, nor any necessity of law as in the events of nature. This act results from a conscious self-determination which confirms the control of the person over his own act and which is situated in a sphere transcending nature.[23]

As a consequence, the free act is incapable of being foreseen in its concrete singularity. ''In regard to free events, it is for the best of reasons that they are incapable of being foreseen. Neither in themselves nor by accident can they be known beforehand in themselves with certitude, their nature being such that they are *absolutely* inamenable to certain foreknowledge, since they depend on no necessity, neither necessity by right nor necessity of fact. For this reason God, though possessing a fully comprehensive knowledge of created wills, nevertheless does not know free decisions in their created causes, that is to say, in the previous disposition of these wills themselves, nor in any other created cause. He knows free human decisions in their state of always being *present* to his divine Vision. And so He knows them with certitude'' (ET, 36). Does this mean that any ''scientific'' study of human action must be declared illegitimate? No, for Maritain is quick to add that free acts ''can, however, be foreseen in a way that is more or less probable, to the

---

[21]　See C, 18-22. This question will be examined in the next chapter.

[22]　''It is possible to show that the human will, which is rooted in the intellect, and which is able to determine itself, or to master the very motive or judgment which determines it and is made efficacious by the will itself, is spiritual in its operation and nature. Every material agent is subject to the universal determinism. Free will is the privilege, the glorious and weighty privilege, of an agent endowed with immaterial power.

''We are responsible for ourselves; we choose for ourselves and decide on our own ends and our own destinies. We are capable of spiritual, supra-sensuous love, and desire and joy, which are naturally intermingled with our organic and sensuous emotions, but which are in themselves affections of the spiritual will, and are awakened through the immaterial light of intellectual insight'' (RR, 58-59).

[23]　*Essays in Thomism,* p. 31. On the complex issue of the relations between natural determinism and freedom, see DK, 28-30, 151-153, 190-192.

extent that one knows the motives that influence free acts or the dispositions, passions, and inclinations of the subject. In this way it is even possible to foresee with a probability approaching certitude the average conduct of a given human multitude in given circumstances. The free act, thus foreseen, will take place *ut in pluribus*" (ET, 36). The sciences of man are therefore possible, but they cannot pretend to a reductive exclusivity according to which the mystery of the person in his free action would be nothing but what is revealed in neutral averages.[24]

Finally, it is useful to remember that the freedom of choice, for Maritain, is situated in the wake of the proper act of the will which is to love and to will the satiating good. The free will then is not completely gratuitous; if it allows the human being to build himself, to attain the perfection of his being, it is through the extension of the gift of nature, the gift that God makes to him of his natural being. Understood in this way, the true meaning of the freedom of choice is found in its relations with the freedom of spontaneity, particularly in its highest form, namely the freedom of perfection, of independence.

IV.- THE CONQUEST OF FREEDOM

"In each of us personality and freedom of independence increase together. For man is a being in movement. If he does not augment, he has nothing, and he loses what he had; he must fight for his being. The entire history of his fortunes and misfortunes is the history of his effort to win together with his own personality, freedom of independence. He is called to the conquest of freedom" (F, 215-216).[25]

Even if man is born the most helpless animal, by virtue of his intellect and free will, it is possible for him to attain to the life of the spirit and to create, so to speak, his being. By virtue of the freedom of choice inscribed in the wake of the spontaneity of his personal nature, man attains to a novel responsibility in the universe of purely material things, the responsibility of giving meaning to his life, to make a life for himself, to conquer his autonomy and his perfection. Initial freedom and the freedom of choice are provided along with the nature of our being as "rational"; we don't have to conquer them. But this freedom of choice should allow us to conquer our terminal freedom; this is our vocation as personal beings.

On the day he was born, the human being was at the lowest level of his freedom. But while his natural being grows, he progressively discovers the aspirations of the person: those of the person in so far as he is human, especially the aspiration toward those freedoms which he can conquer in the

---

[24]   Jeanne PARAIN-VIAL's book, *La Liberté et les sciences de l'homme* (Paris: Privat, 1973), defends a thesis like Maritain's on this question.

[25]   "The person is subsistent and open: and liberty likewise is a power of autonomy and a power of gift. The person is a reality given and a reality still to be achieved: and liberty likewise is a power of choice, inherent and indestructible, and a power to self-fulfilment, which is something that has to be conquered... In this sense, the history of the person is the history of his liberty; the problem of personalization is the problem of liberation." Jean MOUROUX, *The Meaning of Man* (London: Sheed and Ward, 1948), pp. 143-144.

social order; those of the person in so far as he is a person, namely the conquest of freedom in the order of the spiritual life (F, 215-217). This twofold aspiration is inscribed in the depths of the spiritual life (in the spiritual preconscious) according to which the human being is a being capable of understanding and of loving, a communicative being and a communal one.

Starting out then from a situation both precarious and confined, and subject to a desire for a satiating good, the human person is launched in a process of transcendence, certainly relying on natural capabilities and social contributions, and relying particularly on the good use of free will.[26]

The dynamics of the conquest of the freedom of perfection, the process of liberation, must amend a twofold defeat (or limit): "the defeat inflicted by the burden of nature to the aspirations of the person" and "the defeat inflicted to his aspirations by the condition of the creature in the face of divine transcendence" (SP, 132-133). By reason of his bodily condition "the human person is involved in all the miseries and fatalities of material nature, — the servitudes and the needs of the body, heredity, ignorance, selfishness and the savagery of instincts" (SP, 131). In so far as he is a creature, the human person "is not only subject to realities other than himself as to the specifying objects of his knowledge and of his will, but he is also subjected to laws he has not made, as measures regulating his actions" (SP, 131).

Man is indeed a person. "He is a person in the metaphysical root of personality" (SP, 131). But, as a being obscure to himself and to others, and subject to temporal conditions, he must "become what he is", that is, he must progressively conquer his personal being under the double aspect of his inner life and that of his communal life. "Man must win his personality, as well as his freedom, and he pays dearly for it, and runs many risks. He is a person in the order of doing only if his rational energies, and virtues, and love, give such a face to the torrential multiplicity which inhabits him, and freely imprint on him the seal of his radical ontological unity. In this sense, the one knows real personality and real liberty, while the other does not" (SP, 131-132).

In the progressive conquest of his personality, man is subject to the two-sided nature of becoming, which can be actualized in the direction of progress and of liberation, but also in the direction of enslavement. This is the ransom and challenge of the freedom of choice. "There is a false conquest of freedom which is illusory and homicidal. There is a true conquest of freedom which provides truth and life for mankind" (F, 217).[27]

---

[26] "If we lack economic freedom, there is still hope. And the same is true if we lack legal freedom and even political freedom. But if that freedom from which emanate the most personal acts of man is denied, then all the rest becomes immediately empty eloquence and tragic illusion." Francesco VIOLA, "La liberté humaine entre liberté absolue et déterminisme", in *Nova et Vetera*, Geneva, 1976, p. 116.

[27] "Within that invaluable thing which is the person, love works both a death and a resurrection: a death, particularly to one's own egotistical self, which brings freedom from evil and from the tyranny of creatures; and a resurrection which is freedom for the expansion of the human person, a liberty for the integration and realization of his infinite potentialities.

"Nor does love merely spring forth from within the depths of the person, It also goes out to persons, rather than to essences or qualities or ideas." William L. ROSSNER, "Love in the Thought of Jacques Maritain", in *Jacques Maritain, The Man and His Achievement*, p. 239.

Maritain illustrates his analysis of the dynamics of freedom with several examples of this false conquest, in the personal order as well as in the social order. He pauses particularly to show the baneful consequences of the univocalist and immanentist conception according to which freedom allows neither internal variety nor degrees and which turns human freedom into a divine freedom. "In this way of thinking there is neither freedom nor autonomy except in so far as no objective rule or measure is received from a living being other than oneself. And the human person claims for itself then divine freedom" (F, 217). Consequently, an absolute independence of any moral law or the immanent quality of the conscience is asserted, which means the right to "construct morality by himself alone without owing anything to law" (F, 225). The independence of knowledge in relation to being through an idealist conception of science is asserted as well.

This abolition of "wisdom" and the break with God have found their modern expressions, as clear as they are harmful, especially in bourgeois liberalism which viewed religion as "good for the people" and in its antithesis, Marxist Hegelianism which sees in religion "the opium of the people". (F, 225) The social deification of man (in a privileged race) has brought forth Nazi racism. Maritain sees in these two examples — and in several others — a false deification of man, forgetful of the fact that "nature implies basic structures received and determined *ad unum;* these structures are received, they do not originate from the person as the first subject of independent operation; our intellect has a super-physical nature, as does our will" (BT, 235).

In place of that false deification of man, Maritain proposes another kind of "deification", for which it is ultimately in God that the human person must seek to actualize his freedom of perfection; his freedom as his perfection become at once a conquest of man and a gift from God (F, 226-228). Sanctity then becomes the personal ideal to be realized; in this state of perfection, terminal freedom coincides with the plenitude and the perfection of love, the love of God and the love of men. "It is the freedom of God Himself that the perfect spiritual man enjoys, being independent of all external constraint in so far as he depends only on the divine causality, which is extraneous to nothing" (SP, 136).

So, it is in the trajectory leading to God that the process of liberation, taking its departure from the conscious and free life, is located. "Thus, by virtue of a primal free act having the moral good, *bonum honestum,* as its object, a man can tend toward God as the end of his life without knowing God — that is, he then knows God (unconsciously) without knowing Him (consciously)" (RR, 70).[28] This fundamental orientation of man towards God is expressed each time that he performs a free act in conformity with right reason, each time that he chooses the good: "Now, when a man deliberating about his life chooses to love that which is good in itself, the *bonum*

---

[28]   All of chapter six, entitled "The Immanent Dialectic of the First Act of Freedom" (RR, 66-85), deals with this question.

honestum, in order to link his life to it, it is toward God whether he knows it
or not, that he turns himself." (SP, 122).

For Maritain, the highest realization of this liberation is found in the
sanctity which is the fruit of supernatural grace, "a formal participation in the
Divine Nature, in other terms, a deifying life received from God" (F, 226).[29]
Man's personal liberation expresses itself in manifold ways in human history
and reaches its highest peaks in the "natural" mystical experience (for
instance, Indian mystical spirituality) and in "natural" contemplation (e.g.
the impetus of Hellenic wisdom).[30]

If such is really the case, if the human being, in the dynamics of his
freedom wills always to transcend himself and tends — consciously or
unconsciously — toward God[31] (even under the faces of false gods) it is
understandable that he has the possibility and even the temptation to take
himself for God, by losing sight of his natural limitations, and forgetting as
well that as a created being he is dependent on objects of knowledge and on
moral rules.

The will to surpass, the conquest of freedom, personal and social
liberation must follow a long and arduous road, and every human being in
each generation must make his way down the road as others have done; it is
the road of education, it is the road of human history; it is the "historical ideal
of the last two centuries" (F, 218).[32] The freedom of spontaneity of created
beings implies, at every degree, certain conditions of exercise; in this sense,
no created freedom can enjoy absolute independence. On the other hand, only
an active and dynamic acceptance of these *conditions* will allow the human
person to become perfect, to pass from his initial freedom to his freedom of
expansion.

For instance, in the order of the spiritual life, the human intellect cannot
become perfect, direct itself to wisdom (which is its crowning glory), except
in the vital acceptance of its condition as a created spirit bound to a body, and
unless it allows itself to be impregnated by being, first perceived through the
opacity of sense knowledge. For "truth is the conformity of the intellect to
reality...being is the proper object of the intellect and it finds its life and its
liberty in adhering to it" (ASE, 59).[33] This fertilization of the spirit facilitates

---

[29]   "This is called eternal life — which begins obscurely here on earth" (F, 226).

[30]   Aristotle, for instance, shows in the *Nicomachean Ethics*, Book X, Chapter VII, that the
supreme happiness dwells in the contemplative life of the mind so that an existence in accordance
with the mind will be "truly divine". Does not the ideal rest in "the contemplation and service of
God"? *Eudemian Ethics*, 1249b 20.

[31]   "But in actual fact the good which every being desires, even without knowing it, is in
the last analysis self-subsisting Good; and thus, in actual fact, the dynamism of human life,
because it tends toward good and happiness, even if their true countenance is not recognized, tend
implicitly, willy-nilly toward Transcendence" (RR, 98).

[32]   "In fact, the conquest of freedom in the social and political order is the central hope
characterizing the historical ideal of the last two centuries, which has constituted at once their
dynamic urge, their power of truth and of illusion" (F, 218).

[33]   "And truth keeps pace with freedom" (PG, 168).

"Man is not born free unless in the basic potencies of his being: he becomes free, by
warring upon himself and thanks to many sorrows; by the struggle of the spirit and virtue; by
exercising his freedom he wins his freedom. So that at long last a freedom better than he expected
is *given* him. From the beginning to the end it is truth that liberates him" (F, 218).

the acquisition of the different intellectual virtues, whose crowning glory is the wisdom which is "freedom of exultation" (FMW, 34).

On the other hand, in the moral life, personal liberation proceeds by way of the law, "the pedagogue of freedom" (IH, 183). He who, in the wake of his conscience animated by the love of the good, submits to the moral law and embarks on a virtuous life,[34] makes himself capable of overcoming his selfishness and, by self-mastery, becomes capable of an ever greater love. For "law protects freedom and teaches us to practice it. When love follows the path of law it leads through law to emancipation from all servitude, even the servitude of the law" (F, 226).[35] *Ama et fac quod vis*, to use Saint Augustine's phrase. This internalization of the law in the life of the will fosters the fullness of love which is "freedom of autonomy" (FMW, 34).

The conquest of spiritual freedom, inner freedom, must go hand in hand with the conquest of social and political freedoms. Maritain says: "To my way of thinking, the pursuit of freedom is also at the base of the social and political problem" (EW, 336). In order to grow in a normal way, personal freedom requires the exercise of social freedoms provided for it by a beneficent civilization; for "civilized life tends to grant the human person, — that is, the concrete person of each member of the multitude, — an increasingly larger measure of independence from the external and internal constraints of Nature: an independence assured by the economic guarantees of labour and property, by political rights, by civil virtues, and the culture of the mind" (SP, 133).

Maritain readily acknowledges that "the idea of freedom dominates the majority of the great political philosophies of modern times" (FMW, 39). But he considers that some of them have proclaimed the deepest aspirations of the person to freedom while enclosing these aspirations in either an inadequate or an erroneous philosophy. For instance, he maintains that the liberal or individualist conception which held sway in the nineteenth century centres social life on the freedom of choice taken as an end-in-itself; which, ultimately, ends up in the disintegration of the common good and the maximization of individual freedoms in a society "having within it a multitude of bourgeois Ends-in-Themselves with unlimited freedom to own and to trade and to enjoy the pleasures of life" (FMW, 41).

At the opposite end, political philosophers are found intent, not on the freedom of the person, but, on the freedom of the political body, and the greatness of the state; these philosophies inspired by Hegel whose dream would be "the production of a Leviathan dominating the whole earth, to the Freedom of which a multitude of happy slaves will gladly sacrifice their souls" (FMW, 42).

---

[34] "But it is proper to reflection to show distinctly that nothing resembles less genuine freedom than that state in which a being on the contrary is surrendered, without any recourse, to impulsions it cannot control. Then it will be clearly apparent that freedom is inseparable from a certain self-mastery. "Gabriel MARCEL, "La liberté en 1971", in *Les Etudes philosophiques*, January-March, 1975, 1, p. 9.

[35] See also "Le thomisme et la civilisation", in *Revue de philosophie*, 1928, p. 128.

Maritain's social and political philosophy is inspired by a dynamic subordination of the temporal common good to the good of persons and to their freedom of autonomy. This philosophy, both personalist and communal, proposes the realization of a common good which must "aim at securing for the mass of its citizens conditions that are worthy of man and that will put each citizen, thus equipped for the life of reason and of virtue, in the way of advancing toward perfect freedom and of achieving his eternal destiny" (FMW, 44).[36]

Thus, the political task is above all a product of civilization and culture, that is, a product of liberation directed toward the expansion of persons, having its end in the freedom of perfection. The proper movement of politics is "a movement toward a liberation or emancipation consistent with the true aspirations of our being: progressive liberation from the bondage of material nature, not only for the sake of our material welfare, but above all for the development of the life of the spirit within us; progressive liberation from the diverse forms of political bondage (for since man is a 'political animal', our nature would have each one of us participate actively and freely in political life); progressive liberation from the diverse forms of economic and social bondage (for our nature also would have no man exploited by another man, as a tool to serve the latter's own particular good). Maybe man will not become better. At least his state of life will become better. The structures of human life and humanity's conscience will progress" (RM, 27).

It is important to note the humanist and personalist significance of this social philosophy. If society should allow the exercise of personal, familial, civil and political freedoms, if the socio-economic organization should promote the control of nature while respecting the rights of workers (including the right of free organization of unions), it is with a view to the expansion of a properly human life, including, of course, material development (needed by virtue of the psychosomatic unity of the person), but including also and especially "the development of the theoretical and practical activities (artistic and ethical) peculiarly worthy of being called a human development" (RC, 8).[37]

---

[36]   "Confronted with 'bourgeois' liberalism, communism and totalitarian statism, what we need, I do not cease to say, is a new solution, one that is at the same time personalist and communal, one that sees human society as an organization of freedoms." *Confession of Faith* in *The Social and Political Philosophy of Jacques Maritain* (New York: Charles Scribner's Sons, 1955), p. 338.

Maritain sketches the traits of this society which should follow after liberal capitalism and which could be called a personalist democracy: a society of a corporative, guild, authoritative and pluralist type (FMW, 55-73).

[37]   "Culture or civilization is the expansion, the worldly fructification of human life; therefore, it includes not only the *material* development necessary and sufficient to allow us to lead an upright life here below, but also, and particularly, *moral and intellectual* development, the development of the activities of justice and highmindedness, and activities of wisdom, science and art, activities which properly deserve to be called *human* development; and this culture is natural to man on the same terms as the progressive work of reason in him, whose product and achievement it is. It responds to the fundamental wish of human nature, but it is the work of the mind and of freedom joining their efforts to that of nature" (QC, 230).

Truly human development is "mainly intellectual, moral and spiritual development (taking the word *spiritual* in its widest acceptation)" (RC, 2-3). It is located on the trajectory of the life of the mind and of personal freedom which are the specific manifestations of the person.

It is from this perspective that Maritain states, among other things, his philosophy of work and of the rights of the worker, his philosophy of the means of social progress, and his conception of technical progress.

Human work — even the most physical kind — has a liberating significance which has not always been appreciated in the history of mankind. In this respect, Maritain asserts that "the consciousness of self *(prise de conscience)* achieved by the working person and the working community" is an important phenomenon which was produced in the nineteenth century, an historic achievement implying "the consciousness of the dignity of work and of the worker, of the dignity of the human person in the worker as such" (RM, 51).

Human work is not just a commodity. "The work which antiquity most despised, manual work, imposes the forms of reason on matter, and delivers man from the fatalities of material nature (provided however he does not turn his industry into an idol which enslaves him even more); thus, work has a value of natural redemption; it is like a remote prefiguration of the communications of love. Man is both *homo faber* and *homo sapiens,* and he is *homo faber* before being in truth and actually *homo sapiens* and in order to become the latter" (SP, 175).

This liberating value of work as "operation of reason" grows with its value as a service to the community. Work is an essentially human activity born in the heart before passing outside. As such, it inspires the love of a job well done. But this love also stems from the purpose of work, for the activity of working "goes beyond the work it serves, and by an instinct of communication which demands to be perfected in goodness, proceeds to the service of other men. You can give high wages to a workman for work manifestly useless, — for instance, the task which used to be imposed on convicts, of digging holes and then filling them up, — and this workman will be driven to despair. It is essential to human work that it be useful to men" (SP, 174).

It is not superfluous to add that transitive action is inferior to immanent action, and that, however necessary and liberating the activity of work may be, it is subordinated to the dynamics of the inner life.[38] Work has no end in itself, it exists for rest, for active leisure, "that of the culture of the mind and the heart, the joy of knowing, the spiritual delectations which art and beauty offer us, the generous enthusiasm supplied by disinterested love, compassion and communion, zeal for justice, devotion to the commonwealth and to

---

[38] Transitive action "strikes the senses more vividly, because its place is the world of material bodies, and its manifestation is by motion: but it is as much diminution as perfection. Action at its highest is immanent action, the action of thought and of love, proper to perfect living beings and dwelling in them as a pure quality, bearing witness to the independence of their essence" (T, 34).

mankind. The very law of work to which every member of the commonwealth has to submit, demands that all should have access to that leisure" (SP, 180-181).[39]

Work then will be liberating if it is combined with the social rights belonging to each human person: the right to work, to a just wage, to union freedom, to property entitlement (by co-property, co-direction etc.), the right to vacations and to leisure time, the right to unemployment insurance from the community[40], etc.

In the complicated realization of the aims of social life, in the history of civilization, advances are often very slow and hard to achieve, and they are also subject to failure. The temptation can be very strong to use radical means, in the name of promoting human dignity, in order to rectify injustices which cry to heaven, while holding human dignity in contempt. "Aldous Huxley has also denounced the folly of attempting good ends by bad means" (SP, 231).

The means are in a way the end itself in the process of becoming, therefore they must correspond to the end, and it is a very great error to use bad means to attain an intrinsically good end (MS, 55). In the same way, it would be a serious illusion to rely only on means external to man, to rely on technical rationalization alone to achieve human and social progress. "A certain style of pedagogy, a certain orientation of professional life, a certain 'scientific' psychotherapy are other modes of external technique by which anthropocentric humanism tries in vain to react against the inevitable pursuit of freedom in a way that follows from its own principle, namely by the use of technique and not by way of asceticism" (FMW, 95-96).

It is principally by human means, the means which come from man himself, his vital resources, his freedom and his virtues that one should seek to improve the commonwealth. "The establishment of a regime that shall be worthy of the rational nature of man and oriented to his freedom of autonomy postulates the use of means that are worthy of his rational nature and that are consonant with such freedom" (FMW, 164). Technical, economic and political changes, necessary as they may be, can only really be liberating if man has a change of heart at the same time.

This change of heart is all the more pressing as technical progress casts such a spell over minds, that for a goodly number, it becomes the measure of human progress.[41] And yet, that is to be greatly led astray, for "modern

---

[39]   "Everyone must work, or share in the burden of the social community, according to his own ability. But work is not an end in itself; work should afford leisure for the joy, expansion, and delight of the spirit" (C, 89).

[40]   See RM, 92-111.

[41]   "It is from this field of material making that popular imagination borrows its notion of progress: and principally it sees it as something like the increasing rapidity of means of transport — for here also is verified the definition of progress proposed by those learned men who call it 'economy of energy'. Progress of this order has held the stage for roughly a century with a shower of marvels, and the fascination exercised by it has certainly served more than anything else to create the prestige that the dogma of Progress has among men. It would be a waste of time to remind you that of itself it contributes nothing either to the moral perfection of men nor even to their earthly happiness — since concupiscence is limitless and human needs grow faster than the means of satisfying them" (T, 152).

progress" does not always bring with it the expected liberation. In fact, the functionalization of human existence following the invasion of technology and the over-evaluation of economic goods, is accompanied by a weakening of family ties, a weakening of concern for a succeeding generation, the proliferation of psychological and moral disorders, a devaluation of human life (euthanasia, suicide, abortion, etc.). "It is remarkable," Maritain writes, "that a certain conception of the control of nature by man is compensated in the balance sheet, with startling uniformity, by one same single consequence: the cessation of life" (RC, 21).

That doesn't mean that we ought to exclude technology, but we must tame it, make it subject to the human good; instead of asking man to adapt himself to the machine, we should rather "humanize" the machine. "Technique is good — mechanics is good. I disapprove of the spirit of archaism which would suppress the machine and technique. But if mechanics and technique are not mastered, subjected by force to the good of man, that is to say entirely and rigorously subordinated to religious ethics and made instruments of an ascetic morality, humanity is literally lost" (DD, 147).

If progress is the rule in the realm of the material production of the practical sciences, that is, where acquisition is cumulative and constitutes a part of the common inheritance, it isn't necessarily so in the order of the properly spiritual and moral life of man, a life which is subject to endless vicissitudes. It is easier for human beings to dominate external matter — the world of objects — than to master their own being and their own animated matter — their subjectivity (T, 154).

In closing this chapter on human freedom, it will be useful to state several corollaries of Maritain's philosophy of freedom.

"The freedom of choice, the *free will,* is not its own end. It is ordained to the conquest of freedom in the sense of freedom of *exultation* or *autonomy.* And it is in this conquest, demanded by the essential postulates of human personality that the dynamism of freedom consists" (SP, 132).[42] In a certain sense, one can say that free will is the privileged means given to the human creature to dominate nature, and build himself in order to be master of himself and to give of himself.

Even if freedom of choice has its fulfillment in the freedom of perfection, in terminal freedom, it is freer — or more freedom — than the latter since it is not only free of all constraint, but also of any necessity.

On the other hand, the freedom of choice is less perfect than the terminal freedom to which it is ordained, since the *perfection* of the act is better than its free character: "one does not die in the name of free will; one dies in the name of freedom of autonomy or exultation" (SP, 137).

Lastly, let us add that the liberation of the person, the conquest of his freedom of autonomy, is the end of history[43] and that, in a sense, it transcends

---

[42]   "For free-will is a means to liberty, and the power of choosing is there to serve a power to self-achievement." Jean MOUROUX, *The Meaning of Man* (London: Sheed and Ward, 1948), p. 143.

[43]   See PG, 40-41.

history. For, according to Maritain, only autonomy, the liberation of the person as a result of the love of God in the beatific vision, can fully satisfy the human person's desire for freedom. "We assert that the liberation demanded by man is such that the possession of the world would still leave him unsatisfied; we consider man to be an unusual animal, who will be content with nothing less than absolute joy" (SP, 56).

Chapter III

Education for Freedom

Maritain's personalism and his philosophy of freedom reveal to us to some extent the way in which "the face of our birth" is reflected in the aspirations of the person to spiritual (or inner) freedom and to social freedoms; they let us catch a glimpse of the answer he brings to the question: "What is man that he needs to be educated?" Here the basic and dynamic unity of Maritain's thought is manifest; his writings most explicitly devoted to the philosophy of education are in vital continuity with his other works and more particularly with his philosophy of man. The human person is a being of freedom; his education will be or ought to be a process of liberation, and education for freedom.[1]

I.- WHAT IS EDUCATION?

If the human being is educable, he owes it to the fact that he is both a natural and a cultural being. By his nature — as an individual — he is born devoid of the most elementary means of subsistence, he is born "prematurely"; he is subject to those who gave him birth and to the society without which his life would not only be precarious, but without a future. Yet, by virtue of his nature as a "rational animal", he possesses an intellect and a free will by which, taking into account his biological, psychological, moral and social becoming, he could become more or less master of his own destiny; he could actively participate in the world of culture, in the world of human creativity in its manifold expressions ranging from the transformation of the material world to the higher forms of social life and the works of the mind (e.g. the arts and literature, political life, religion and so forth). By the good use of his freedom of choice, he will be able to progressively realize his personal and social being, his autonomy, his perfection and to conquer his spiritual freedom and his social freedoms.

The condition of the human being as a natural and a cultural being nevertheless makes him a tributary of the becoming of society and civilization

---

[1] "What he says more comprehensively in these writings is that philosophy of education depends on philosophy of man, and that education is, above all, liberation." Leo R. WARD, "Maritain's Philosophy of Education", in *Jacques Maritain, The Man and His Achievement*, p. 193.

in his own development. The human infant does not inherit directly the social conquests of freedom and civilization; as a personal being, he is born *tabula rasa;* the equipment he inherits does not include the knowledge acquired by his parents, it does not include their intellectual and moral virtues, nor their freedom of autonomy. That is why "man cannot progress in his own specific life, both intellectually and morally, without being helped by collective experience previously accumulated and preserved, and by a regular transmission of acquired knowledge' (C, 2), and the importance of education comes from that fact.

The human being can only conquer his freedom by actively sharing in the human tradition. Moreover this dialectic of the relations between human becoming and social life, and between freedom and tradition confronts us with the basic question of authority in education, that is, the question of the relationship between the educator and the person to be educated, between authority and freedom (this question will be examined in part three of this chapter). Man is an historical animal. "In order to reach self-determination, for which he is made, he needs discipline and tradition, which will both weigh heavily on him and strengthen him so as to enable him to struggle against them — which will enrich that very tradition — and the enriched tradition will make possible new struggles, and so forth," (C, 2).

Our primary responsibility, then, is to "become what we are"; it is why education, taken in its broadest and most inclusive sense, refers "to any process whatsoever by means of which man is shaped and led toward fulfillment" (C, 2). "Thus the chief task of education is above all to shape man, or to guide the evolving dynamism through which man forms himself as a man" (C, 1), put in another way, to prepare the child and the adolescent to teach themselves all their life long. According to this approach, there is no antinomy between *being educated* and *educating oneself;* the one achieves its purpose in the other and the overall process of education includes both. A human being cannot suitably take upon itself the process of self-education unless it is first educated. It is why Maritain recognizes that, beyond the broader meaning of education mentioned earlier, the word education has two other meanings: either "the task of formation which adults intentionally undertake with regard to youth, or, in its strictest sense, the special task of schools and universities" (C, 2). These two meanings are distinct although complementary and indeed they often overlap with each other.

In the face of the challenge that education represents as a process of human becoming (the coming to be of a complete and concrete man), certain deviations which would risk falsifying its direction must be guarded against, especially the basic error which consists in disregarding the aims of education as well as the error of reducing the aims of education to fit a truncated conception of man. "Education is an ethical art (or rather a practical wisdom in which a determinate art is embodied). Now every art is a dynamic trend toward an object to be achieved, which is the aim of this art. There is no art without ends, art's very vitality is the energy with which it tends toward its end" (C, 2-3).

Never before have educators had at their disposal pedagogical means as numerous and diverse as those they have today. Thanks to the offices of guidance counsellors with the instruments of educational psychology (sets of all kinds of tests etc.), the contemporary educator can know in a rather precise way the tastes and talents of pupils or students; he can have at his disposition a multiplicity of educational materials (audio-visual materials, attractive books etc.). We all know the hopes of democratizing education and of pedagogical innovations based on educational technology and on computer learning.[2]

These educational means are not bad, "on the contrary, they are generally much better than those of the old pedagogy" (C, 3). Still their use incurs risks which are not to be minimized; in fact these means are so good that they make one lose sight of the aim of education, and that, according to Maritain, is the principal reproach one can make against contemporary pedagogy where the vital efficacy of education "is replaced by a process of infinite multiplication, each means developing and spreading for its own sake" (C, 3).

This is not a criticism of a purely theoretical order; it is related to concrete situations. In fact, "the child is so well tested and observed, his needs so well detailed, his psychology so clearly cut out, the methods for making it easy for him everywhere so perfected, that the end of all these commendable improvements runs the risk of being forgotten or disregarded" (C, 3). Maybe there is some truth in this witty remark of Maritain: "Moreover, by dint of insisting that in order to teach John mathematics it is more important to know John that to know mathematics — which is true enough in one sense — the teacher will so perfectly succeed in knowing John that John will never succed in knowing mathematics" (C, 13-14).

It is why the more educational means are perfected and made more complex — which is an improvement — the more their employment requires "a parallel strengthening of practical wisdom and of the dynamic trend toward the goal" (C, 4).[3] For the means are the ends in the process of becoming. To forget the purpose of education in order to give all one's attention to the perfection of the means of education then can have very serious consequences.

No less harmful would be a pedagogy inspired by too narrow a vision of man. "It should be pointed out that if we tried to build education on the single pattern of the scientific idea of man and carry it out accordingly, we could only do so by distorting or warping this idea" (C, 5). In fact (as was explained in the first chapter), the sciences constitute a precious contribution

---

[2] On this topic, see E. FAURE, *Learning to Be*, pp. 116-133.

[3] "That is why it is an error to maintain that objective pedagogy and normative pedagogy vary inversely; in fact, they vary directly, the second mobilizing the will to organize the first and preceding it by furnishing its objectives to it. Finally, if there are no sciences, philosophy is impotent, for want of knowing if its ends can be obtained, and how; but if there is no philosophy, the sciences are inhibited, for want of knowing on what to bring their techniques to bear. Far from being opposed or in competition, both are required together; their double rise cannot be dissociated and they function by way of mutual stimulation." Guy AVANZINI, *Introduction aux sciences de l'éducation* (Toulouse: Privat, 1976), p. 113.

to the knowledge of man (by the study of biological, psychological, and social phenomena, etc.), but by definition they cannot throw any light on the values of the person as such.[4]

The education of the human person is a "human awakening"; it implies a human ideal, which ought, insofar as it is possible to do so, take into account the whole man. And philosophy, in spite of its misadventures, can greatly assist us in this task.[5] For the goal of education in the broadest sense "is to help a child of man attain his full formation or his completeness as a man" (EM, 50). This education lasts a lifetime, since we have never finished being born to the human, we have never finished conquering our freedom of perfection.

This "full formation of man" takes into account the psychosomatic unity of the human being and includes the multiple dimensions of the person in an integrative perspective: physical culture, emotional development, intellectual work and socialization. The objective of education is the expansion of the human person in the perspective of an integral humanism: "an integral education for an integral humanism" (C, 88).[6] Moreover, in order to respect the wholeness of the constituents of the person, education must foster their development while taking into consideration the particular traits of the individual: his age, his talents, the cultural environment, etc. "The job of education is not to shape the Platonist man-in-himself, but to shape a particular child belonging to a given nation, a given social environment, a given historical age" (C, 1).

To sum up, the objective of education is "to guide man in the evolving dynamism through which he shapes himself as a human being — armed with knowledge, strength of judgment, and moral virtues — while at the same time conveying to him the spiritual heritage of the nation and the civilization in which he is involved, and preserving in this way the century-old achievements of generations" (C, 10).

This does not mean that everything is of equal importance and that each educational act has to be addressed to every component of the person. The school, for instance, has a role of its own and "it is more concerned with intelligence and knowledge than with the will and moral virtues" (EM, 144); but in the fulfillment of this noble task, the school should respect the wholeness of the person and constitute a learning environment favourable for his integral expansion.

---

[4]   In *Freedom in the Modern World,* Maritain, taking inspiration from Pascal's *Pensées,* recalls that we must respect in man the different orders which are present in him and their hierarchy; "the order of bodies subserves that of soul or Spirit, and this latter subserves the order of Charity" (pp. 77-78).

[5]   "Human nature does not change, but our knowledge of it may be philosophically warped or inadequate" (EM, p. 52). "If the aim of education is the helping and guiding of man toward his own human achievement, education cannot escape the problems and entanglements of philosophy, for it supposes by its very nature a philosophy of man..." (C, 4).

[6]   See also *Education of Man,* pages 130-133. "We must take education in its total sense; mutilate it and you mutilate man." O. REBOUL, *La philosophie de l'éducation* (Paris: P.U.F., 1976), p. 11.

If everything is not of equal importance in education, what are its primary purposes?

II.- THE PRIMARY GOALS OF EDUCATION

Perhaps the leveling of values, and as a result, their devaluation, is one of the greatest sorrows of our time. If the outpourings of the advertising used by our consumer society were to be believed, very little would be sufficient to make us happy. It even seems that this tendency toward leveling has reached certain educational circles where the student can obtain a diploma cheaply provided that he has accumulated a certain number of selected courses — according to his talents and tastes, as we say — in the showcase of optional courses[7] offered by the school to him; in order to achieve this objective of offering more and more numerous optional courses, larger and ever larger schools are built in which "mass production" becomes the rule and where the atmosphere is anonymous. Like the society which produces it, it gives favored treatment to the freedom of choice to the detriment of more basic values. With the assistance of pluralist ideology, it is easy to end up considering everything as of equal value, or better, to adopt a neutral attitude in the face of values. Then, utility gains the upper hand and so the outcome is a false hierarchy of values.

For, is it really possible to educate, to educate oneself without a certain hierarchy of values and remaining neutral?[8] For Maritain, education is a human development and this development must surely actualize the whole man in unity (according to his nature) and taking into consideration what is the most important thing in him. "There is no unity or integration without a stable hierarchy of values" (EM, 53).

Consequently, education (both in the broad and in the narrow sense of the term) as a process of becoming must aim at the actualization of the whole man but by focusing on what is the most important thing in him, which does not mean neglecting or forgetting what is of secondary importance. So Maritain is logically led to articulate the primary goals of education which are, in descending order of importance: *first,* the conquest of inner freedom; *second,* the social development of the person. The other dimensions of the person are not neglected for all that, on the contrary, for "in such a hierarchy of values what is infravalent is not sacrificed to, but kept alive by, what is supravalent" (EM, 54).

A. THE CONQUEST OF INTERNAL FREEDOM

"Thus the prime goal of education is the conquest of internal and spiritual freedom to be achieved by the individual person, or, in other words,

---

[7] "Of course, the rejection of the elective system does not imply that in addition to the essential (and therefore required) subjects of the curriculum other subjects should not be taught in optional courses, chosen by students according to their own preferences" (C, 65fn.).

[8] "To admit complete neutrality amounts to renouncing education." O. REBOUL, *L'endoctrinement* (Paris: P.U.F., 1977), p. 63. All of Chapter Three (pp. 53-72) entitled "Atteinte à la neutralité?" bears on this question.

his liberation through knowledge and wisdom, good will, and love'' (C, 11)[9]. The human being does not exist merely as a physical being; by reason of his personal being, ''there is in him a richer and nobler existence; he has spiritual superexistence through knowledge and love'' (C, 8).[10] The intellect and the will are what is most important in the development of the person. They are the basic dynamisms placed in operation in the progressive realization of his own being, in the pursuit of human perfection, in the conquest of autonomy and of personal expansion.

The noble task of conquering the freedom of expansion — or the personality — is then a primary requirement of the human person and the fundamental aspirations for freedom take the form of ''the desire for internal and spiritual freedom''. In the demands for a democratic education, is there not something of an echo of this aspiration?'' A democratic education is an education which helps human persons to shape themselves, judge by themselves, to love and to prize high truths which are the very root and safeguard of their dignity, to respect in themselves and in others human nature and conscience, and to conquer themselves in order to win their liberty'' (EM, 158).[11]

The quality of our democratic societies depends more on the richness of the personal life of its citizens than on their ''functional'' competence (which is not for that reason to be neglected). A true democracy requires enlightened, *autonomous* citizens, and therefore, an education based on the conquest of a genuine autonomy of persons. On the other hand, autonomous citizens will make the human city more fraternal and more genuinely democratic, that is, respectful of persons and of their freedoms.

The spiritual or internal freedom to be conquered by education is not identical with the spontaneity of the instincts, for ''I may develop along the lines of individuality, that is, toward the letting loose of the tendencies which are present in me by virtue of matter and heredity'' (C, 39). Such a surrender would only disperse the human individual, by subjecting him to the slavery of desires and passions; far from leading to his liberation (fruition of a movement of self-overcoming), it would degrade the human individual by rendering him the slave of determinisms which are in him by reason of his materiality. ''If

---

[9] ''For Maritain, education is above all a liberation. Its primary aim is not to mold men as a function of the interests of the polity, but to prepare them and to assist them to conquer true freedom, the freedom of autonomy. It is not that freedom which all men normally enjoy when they carry out their roles in a well run society and which entails independence, the possibility of expression and expansion; education must also lead to that, but that is not its essential task. The freedom on its horizon is above all internal and spiritual, the full development of the person in that which is most personal to him.'' Joseph DE FINANCE, ''La philosophie de la liberté chez Maritain'', in *Recherches et Débats*, #19 (Paris: Fayard, 1957), pp. 113-114.

[10] That is why Maritain's philosophy of freedom (already examined in Chapter II) is so important for his philosophy of education. ''The doctrine of the conquest of freedom is at the heart of Maritain's educational theory...'' D. and I. GALLAGHER, introduction to *The Education of Man*, p. 25.

[11] ''Education is education for freedom. And the world within which it has to fulfill its duties is sick with a frustrated longing for freedom and beauty, and has unlearned the primary conditions and requirements of freedom'' (EM, 101).

the development occurs in the direction of material individuality, it will be oriented towards the detestable ego whose law is to *grasp* or absorb for itself. At the same time personality as such, will tend to be adulterated and to dissolve" (PCG, 44). The interior life can only grow to the extent that the life of reason and freedom dominate the life of the instincts, presupposing a certain self-mastery.[12] Perhaps this is one of the hardest problems in education, for how can a human being expand himself and give of himself if he doesn't learn at the same time to master himself?

The role of education is not the conquest of free will "which is a gift of nature in each of us, and which is also — it is important to recall it — the privileged means of realizing the person.[13] The primary essential aim of education is located in the conquest of the freedom "which is expansion and autonomy", as a response to the deepest yearnings of the person, that is to say, in the unceasing development of the intellect and the will by the progressive acquisition of the intellectual and the moral virtues.[14] Education has as its end the conquest of "spontaneity whose highest form is spiritual autonomy" (BPT, 263).

Here again, according to Maritain, there is a serious mistake to be avoided. For the freedom which is at issue "is not a mere unfolding of potentialities without any object to be grasped, or a mere movement for the sake of movement, without aim or objective to be attained... A movement without aim is just moving around in circles and getting nowhere" (C, 11). Spiritual activities are *intentional* activities; the intellect can only develop itself and become liberating by internalizing the object (the truth), even if imperfectly attained. The will can only attain its perfection through the love of the good.

There is more than one ambiguity in certain educational expressions, for instance: *Learn to learn,* or *being in the process of searching*. Of course, they contain an important truth if the intention is to indicate the emptiness of reducing knowledge to a "possession of the truth," perfectly grasped once and for all and enclosed so to speak — encapsulated — in several ready made formulations. For the multiform universe of truth can only be understood in a fragmentary and approximating way. "The aim, here on earth, will always be grasped in a partial and imperfect manner, and in this sense, indeed, the movement is to be pursued without end. Yet the aim will somehow be grasped, even though partially" (C, 11). And then it is certain that the human

---

[12]   "Man can become master of his nature by imposing the law of reason — of reason aided by grace — on the universe of his own inner energies. That work, which in itself is a construction in love, requires that our branches be pruned to bear fruit; a process called mortification. Such a morality is an ascetic morality" (DD, 146).

[13]   Perhaps it is the illusion of supporters of complete permissiveness to believe that this freedom of choice can by itself, without any assistance, realize the difficult task of being born to the human...

[14]   Too often, by reason of a Jansenist or Manichean outlook, the virtues are perceived as "strait jackets" and not as factors of liberation, and the "virtuous person" perceived as "dead" to this world and not as a real living being.

being must become skilled in learning by himself if he wants to continue teaching himself throughout his life.

However, if *Learn to learn* merely means "the development of the strength, skill, and accuracy of man's mental powers, whatever the thing to be learned may be" (C, 51), then, from Maritain's viewpoint, such a formulation becomes unacceptable. The process of searching which would not be rooted in presuppositions and wouldn't nourish any hope, even the slightest one, of attaining some truth would be devoid of any meaning. For "it is not by the gymnastics of its [the mind's] faculties, it is by truth that it is set free, when truth is really known, that is, vitally assimilated by the insatiable activity which is rooted in the depths of self" (C, 52).[15]

The liberation of the intellect therefore results primarily from the internalization of its object, the truth which does not depend on us, but on that which is. "Truth is an infinite realm — as infinite as being — whose wholeness transcends infinitely our powers of perception, and each fragment of which must be grasped through vital and purified internal activity. This conquest of being, this progressive realization of the ever-growing and ever-renewed significance of truths already attained, opens and enlarges our mind and life, and really situates them in freedom and autonomy" (C, 12).

This dependence on the truth that sets us free is at the very principle of human action as such, at the principle of its specifically human effectiveness. To see in human knowledge as pure pragmatism does only "an organ of response to the actual stimuli and situations of the environment" would be to reduce it to an animal kind of knowledge. The activity of thinking begins with an intuition, not with a question or a difficulty. "At the beginning of human action, insofar as it is human, there is truth, grasped or believed to be grasped for the sake of truth. Without trust in truth, there is no human effectiveness. Such is, to my mind, the chief criticism to be made of the pragmatic and instrumentalist theory of knowledge" (C, 13). The possibility of *understanding* and afterwards of exercising a free act, that is an act that is conscious and thoughtful — the possibility of acting in a human and personal way — springs from the capacity that the human intellect has to *perceive* being.

Moreover, there are kinds of knowledge which are more important and more vital than others; there is a hierarchy of values in the intellectual life. "In the intellectual realm, wisdom, which knows things eternal and creates order and unity in the mind, is superior to science or to knowledge through particular causes; and the theoretical intellect, which knows for the sake of knowing, comes before the practical intellect, which knows for the sake of action" (EM, 53-54).[16] The higher kinds of knowledge are the most

---

[15] "But to live in a state of doubt as regards, not phenomena, but the ultimate realities the knowledge of which is a natural possibility, privilege, and duty for human intelligence, is to live more miserably than animals, which at least tend with instinctive and buoyant certitude towards the ends of their ephemeral life" (C, 116-117).

[16] "The curcial error is that of holding that nothing is any more important than anything else, that there can be no order of goods and no order in the intellectual realm. There is nothing central and nothing peripheral, nothing primary and nothing secondary, nothing basic and nothing superficial." Robert Hutchins quoted in *Education at the Crossroads*, p. 54.

liberating kinds. This is why an education for freedom must be directed toward wisdom. Maritain is largely inspired by this principle in his statements on curricula.[17]

The true aspirations to freedom by reason of the will — whose act is also *intentional* — find their way in the love of the good; their realization and their transcendence are situated on the curve of an ever more perfect love of an ever greater good. "And speaking of will and love rather than knowledge, no one is freer, or more independent, than the one who gives himself for a cause or a real being worthy of the gift" (C, 12).

Now "love does not regard ideas or abstractions or possibilities, love regards existing persons" (C, 96). The rectitude of the will and love are not taught, they are lived starting with the gift made by the author of nature. In this regard, Maritain recalls the privileged role of the family for fostering the budding of love. "Is not family love the primary pattern of any love uniting a community of men?" (C, 96). It is likewise by friendship, discipline, trials and so forth that love is deepened and that the moral virtues flourish; this school of life is all the more important since, as Aristotle said, "to know does little, or even nothing, for virtue" (C, 95).

By the education of the intellect and of the will, the human being then can conquer his personality, his internal and spiritual freedom. "In so far as it relates to the life of the intellect it is wisdom and the full possession of spiritual life, freedom of exultation...; in so far as this adhesion relates to the life of the will, it is the plenitude of perfect love and freedom of autonomy. Of these two aspects, the first will appear in its perfect form only in the vision of God, the second has priority in our present life: they are nevertheless inseparable" (FMW, 34).

In the process of personal growth, therefore, the development of the intellect and that of the will, whose mutual overlapping we are aware of in the free act, should not be isolated or unduly separated. It is why any intellectualist or voluntarist theory of education strongly risks compromising the liberating character of education.

In this regard, Maritain rejects at the start "a certain form of intellectualism [which] seeks the supreme achievements of education in sheer dialectical or rhetorical skill" (C, 18), for, as was shown earlier,[18] this pure gymnastics of the mind forgets the liberating power of truth; it contributes little to enlighten the person on the meaning to give to his life. It can form minds skilled in discussion and direct them more towards sophistry than towards wisdom. The consequence of this first form of intellectualism is that nothing is more important than anything else in the life of the mind and that finally nothing is important at all. "We are facing there a result of the fact that too often contemporary education has deemed it suitable to substitute

---

[17]   See especially C, 66-75 and EM, 69-82. "Education directed toward wisdom, centered on the humanities, aiming to develop in people the capacity to think correctly and to enjoy truth and beauty, is education for freedom, or liberal education" (EM, 69).

[18]   See pp. 55-56.

training-value for knowledge-value in other words, mental gymnastics for truth, and being in fine fettle, for wisdom'' (C, 54-55).[19]

The second form of intellectualism which Maritain challenge is the kind which "seeks the supreme achievements of education in scientific and technical specialization'' (C, 18). This insistence on the "working and experiential'' functions of the intellect may appear at first glance to be the necessary corollary of technological progress and the invasion of modern life by technique.[20] Yet, "an educational program which would aim at forming specialists ever more perfect in ever more specialized fields, and unable to pass judgment on any matter that goes beyond their specialized competence, would lead indeed to a progressive animalization of the human mind and life (C, 19). In fact, the animal is a specialist and can only be that; we may marvel with good reason while watching a bird make its nest, the bee producing a delicious honey, but what is natural and perfect in the animal guided by instinct is not sufficient to make man more human. "The overwhelming cult of specialization dehumanizes man's life'' (C, 19).[21]

Such a dehumanization endangers the very foundations of democracy; ultimately an educational system based exclusively on specialization (and professional orientation), such a "process of differentiation of the bees in the human beehive'', would quickly transform democracy into a kind of state technocracy in which the specialists in political science alone would have a sure competence in the realm of political activity and people would be unable to pass any judgment outside of its own particular field of specialization.

On the other hand, the very demands for technological competence have quickly led to the understanding that "man's fine ingenuity strengthened by an education which liberates and broadens the mind is of as great import as technical specialization, for out of these free resources of human intelligence there arises, in managers and workers, the power of adapting themselves to new circumstances and mastering them'' (C, 20).[22] Therefore, the intellectualism of extreme specialization is insufficient by itself to educate man.

If intellectualism can dehumanize the human person and prevent his liberation, the consequences of voluntarism in education are hardly more positive.

---

[19] Would it be for the same reason that in certain circles logic becomes the compass of philosophy and that philosophy has no more importance than any other subject, no matter what?

[20] The Report of the Faure Commission reveals a good deal of optimism regarding the liberating capabilities of scientific knowledge and technology. In this regard, it seems to us that Maritain's position approaches that of Alain." See in this context Georges PASCAL, *Alain éducateur* (Paris: P.U.F., 1969) pp. 56-60.

[21] "It is a pity to see so many young people bewildered by highly developed and specialized, but chaotic, instruction about anything whatever in the field of particular sciences and miserably ignorant of everything that concerns God and the deepest realities in man and the world. What we are faced with, in this regard, is a kind of regular frustration — by adults and the general organization of teaching — of certain of the most vital needs and aspirations, and even of the basic rights, of intellectual nature in young persons" (EM, 55).

[22] "The aim (of education) is manhood, not manpower." Robert M. HUTCHINS, *The Learning Society* (London: Pall Mall Press, 1968), p. 91.

The voluntarism that Maritain condemns comes garbed in different forms, whether it concerns a kind of "irrational"[23] training or whether it is a matter of what is called the education of the will, the education of character building. These forms share in common a contempt for the intellect. In spite of all the good will of the schools which have set themselves the mission of "refitting and vitalizing the wills", generally, the results, according to Maritain, have been disappointing. "Character is something easily warped or debased, difficult to shape" (C, 21). Neglecting the formation of the intellect by concentrating on the formation of the will makes all kinds of fanaticism and intolerance possible and imprisons the person rather than liberating him.

Voluntarism recalls a truth disregarded by intellectualism, namely that "the main point is surely to be a good man rather than to be a learned man" (C, 20). Nevertheless, it is not possible to become an upright man unless the moral life is truly internalized, that is, unless it finds its source in an enlightened conscience. Our personal life cannot be confined to the intellectual life, but without the intellectual life, our life would not be human.

We have already presented Maritain's position in regard to the respective value of the intellect and of the will.[24] "Intelligence is in and by itself nobler than the will of man, for its activity is more immaterial and universal. But we believe also that, in regard to the things or the very objects on which this activity bears, it is better to will and love the good than simply to know it" (C, 22). It is important to make both the intellect and the will advance simultaneously in order to liberate the person, but "the shaping of the will is throughout more important to man than the shaping of the intellect" (C, 22).[25]

If it is true that the vital factor of education is the energy with which it tends toward its end, education will be liberating in so far as it is based on the life of the mind, to the extent to which the inner life of the person will grow. "The whole function of this act is to prune and trim — operations in which both the individual and the person are interested — in such wise that, within the intimacy of the human being, the gravity of individuality diminishes and that of true personality, and its generosity increases. Such an art, to be sure, is difficult" (PCG, 46).[26]

---

[23]   "I mean in the effectiveness of Nazi training, schools, and youth organizations, in smashing all sense of truth in human minds and in perverting the very function of language and morally devastating the youth and making the intellect only an organ of the technical equipment of the state" (C, 21).

[24]   See page 24.

[25]   "Along with the Aristotelian school, Maritain has always taught that the intellect in itself, by its superior level of immanence and immateriality, is nobler than the will. But he has also taught along with Christianity that love is worth more than intelligence, at least when its object is higher than man, for "considering the things we know, these things exist in us by knowledge according to the mode of existence and the dignity of our own soul", while the things we love "attract us to them according to their own mode of existence and their own dignity". Henry BARS, "Sujet et subjectivité selon Jacques Maritain", in *Les Études philosophiques*, January-March, 1975, pp. 43-44.

[26]   "Man will be fully a person, a *per se subsistens* and a *per se operans*, only in so far as the life of reason and liberty dominates that of the senses and passions in him; otherwise he will remain like the animal, a simple *individual*, the slave of events and circumstances, always led by

Finally, this inner freedom should not be understood as a "closed" freedom; the more the human person reaches spiritual freedom "by knowledge and wisdom, good will and love", the more he understands his solidarity with other persons, and the more he is apt to participate in social life.

B. The Development of the Person in the Social Sphere

If "the primary end of education concerns the human person in his personal life and in his spiritual progress" (CD, 61), the secondary end — and equally essential — concerns the social life of the person.

An education of a individualist type cannot answer to the aspirations of the person as a communicative being and as a communal being. That is why Maritain judges very harshly the education centred exclusively on the person in abstraction from his social environment. "The old education is to be reproached for its abstract and bookish individualism" (C, 16).[27]

As the human person needs social life by reason of his wretchedness as well as by reason of his greatness, by reason of his poverty as well as by reason of his wealth, and since he is both a political and a historical animal, the integral educational process implies "the development of the human being in the social sphere, awakening and strengthening both his sense of freedom and his sense of obligation and responsibility" (C, 14-15).

Moreover the opening to the social dimension is one of the advances realized by education in recent times. "To have made education more experiential, closer to concrete life and permeated with social concerns from the very start is an achievement of which modern education is justly proud" (C, 16). But it is difficult to maintain a balance in everything; now it is rather the danger of an education completely immersed in social ends which confronts us. There is a strong temptation to want to direct education toward social ends and to consider society as the primary aim of culture and the school system. Following such a conception, the school could either become an instrument in the service of the state (of whatever kind it may be) in order

---

something else, incapable of guiding himself; he will be only a part, without being able to aspire to be a whole...

"To develop one's *individuality* is to live the egoistical life of the passions, to make oneself the centre of everything, and end finally by being the slave of a thousand passing goods which bring us a wretched momentary joy.

"*Personality*, on the contrary, increases as the soul rises above the sensible world and by intelligence and will binds itself more closely to what makes the life of the spirit." R. Garrigou-Lagrange, *Le sens commun* (Paris: Nouvelle Librairie nationale, 3rd edition, 1922). Quoted by Maritain, in *Three Reformers*, p. 24.

[27] "Let us say that the Christian City is as fundamentally anti-individualist as it is fundamentally personalist" (TR, 23).

It is worthwhile recalling that Western Christianity has been marked for a long time by a form of individualism which it tried to cast off for almost a century and the Second Vatican Council has clearly moved away from it.

to perpetuate its existence or a means of enslavement in the service of an ideology.[28]

When all is said and done, it does seem vain to oppose personal education to social education; the two forms are needed as essential components of an education for freedom. But in effect to give the the primacy to the social aims of education over its personal aims would entail the subordination of the person with what is most precious to him — truth and freedom — to the society.

One of the consequences of this "sociologism" could be the enslavement of persons to the ends of the state and the negation — or at least the reduction to a minimum — of the autonomous inner life of the person. Another possible consequence of the subordination of personal ends to the social ends of education is "social utilitarianism" which moreover is rediscovered in different degrees in our so-called liberal societies, a utilitarianism which consists, for instance, in giving a priority in the school to learning a trade over personal formation, that is, a priority given to the immediate preparation for social integration to the great detriment of the deep-seated aspirations of the person. This does not mean that "the utilitarian aspect of education which enables the youth to get a job and make a living" (C, 10) ought to be disdained, but we should not forget that the formation of the mind is still more important, and that utility cannot replace the personal values of truth. We should imitate Socrates for whom "the passion for truth had taken the place of the passion for success".[29]

Thus, the education for spiritual freedom is primordial if the intent is to foster the emergence or the perfecting of a democratic society of a personalist kind, for such a society is based on the human qualities of the persons who make it up, on their deep-seated autonomy; and "the role of the instincts, of the feelings, of the irrational is even greater in social and political than in individual life. It follows, therefore, that a work of education, taming the irrational to reason and developing the moral virtues must constantly be pursued within the political body" (RM, 55-56).[30] In fact, "personal freedom itself is as the core of social life, and [...] a human society is veritably a group of human freedoms which accepts obedience and self-sacrifice and a common law for the general welfare, in order to enable

---

[28] In *Pedagogy of the Oppressed*, Paulo Freire warns revolutionary leaders to be on guard against the temptation of making the revolution for the people and not *with* the people, which would be, in his understanding, a new form of alienation. A true revolution, *with* the people, presupposes a humanistic education. See especially pp. 176-186.

[29] Jacques MARITAIN, *Moral Philosophy*, p. 6. "Irrational respect for social taboos is shaken by the same blow (and more effectively than by the arguments of the Sophists). They lose the power on which political conservatism depends most heavily, the power of authority blindly accepted. If they are not founded on reason they are nothing. Nothing keeps things in their place but truth" *(ibid.)*.

[30] "If the development of machinery and the great conquests which we have seen in the realm of matter and technique demand 'an increment of soul' in order to become true instruments of liberation, it is also by means of this increment of soul that democracy will be realized. Its progress is bound up with the spiritualization of secular existence" (CD, 66).

each of these freedoms to reach in everyone a truly human fulfillment'' (C, 15).

On the other hand, personal freedom can only be realized in a social life in which political freedoms, economic freedoms and social freedoms are sacred. For this reason ''it is clear that for the educational body as well as for the individual citizen, freedom, rights and autonomy have responsibility, duties, and moral obligations as their correlatives'' (C, 98).

Finally, if personal liberation can only be achieved in a just and fraternal social life, ''education for the commonwealth supposes the education for the person as prerequisite'' (C, 15), the education for inner spiritual freedom. For this education ''is the inner centre, the living source of personal conscience in which originate idealism and generosity, the sense of law and the sense of friendship, respect for others, but at the same time deeprooted independence with regard to common opinion'' (C, 16).

The dynamics of freedom must respond to the aspirations of the person for spiritual freedom and for social freedoms. The education whose job is ''to guide the evolving dynamism through which man forms himself as a man'' (C, 1) will only be truly human if it is an education for personal freedom and for social responsibility. Even if the first does not exist without the second, and even if the two tasks are essential, the primary purpose of education is the spiritual freedom of the person, and the secondary purpose is social freedom and social responsibility.

III.- SELF-EDUCATION OR EDUCATION BY ANOTHER?

The human person needs an education whose primary — but not exclusive — essential aims are precisely the aims of the person, that is to say, the conquest of spiritual freedom, ''through knowledge and wisdom, good will, and love'', and secondly the conquest of the great social virtues.

Now, it is clear that those properly human actions which constitute the educational process of the person are essentially ''immanent'' activities, internal activities and, as a result, cannot be imposed upon the person from outside. The search for truth, growth in wisdom, the assumptions of one's social responsibilities and a contribution to the advancement of the commonwealth cannot be achieved by the ''interposition of anyone else''. Pedagogical language states very well this fundamental demand of education by using the expression ''internalize''; there is no true education without internalization. In other words, the educational process in essence as in its purpose is a process of self-education and self-liberation.

This means that the primary dynamic factor of education is the internal vitality of the person to be educated, whether young or adult; education is based primarily on the inner resources of the learner. ''The actual merit of modern conceptions of education since Pestalozzi, Rousseau and Kant, has been the rediscovery of the fundamental truth that the principal agent and dynamic factor is not the art of the teacher but the inner principle of activity, the inner dynamism of nature and of the mind'' (C, 32). Consequently every pedagogy which insists on the internal freedom of the child, and on his inner vitality, and is centred on them, is from this viewpoint a good pedagogy.

Does this mean that the contribution of the teacher (parent, school-teacher, professor) should not be considered as important and even necessary in education? At first glance it might seem superfluous to have a teacher in order to educate a human being, endowed with freedom, for freedom. According to Maritain, we must avoid making a serious mistake here.

In fact, a pedagogy of complete permissiveness, without either teacher or law, would risk leading to childishness and passive indifference. "Strangely enough, we may wonder whether an education which yields itself to the sovereignty of the child, and which suppresses any obstacle to be overcome, does not result in making students both indifferent and too docile, too passively permeable to anything the teacher is saying" (C, 32). Moreover, one may doubt whether any such pedagogy can really exist in a pure state.[31]

For, within the human child, there is the spontaneity of the instincts; there is particularity — and it is because of this that he is able to be educated — "the spontaneity of a human and rational nature, and this largely undetermined spontaneity has its inner principle of final determination only in reason, which is not yet developed in the child" (C, 33), "whose intellect, before being fecundated by sense — perception and sense-experience, is but a *tabula rasa,* as Aristotle put it" (C, 30). Knowledge is not the simple reminiscence of a knowledge pre-existing in the soul, following an amnesia of eternal ideas previously contemplated. And the teacher really possesses a knowledge which the student lacks. It is not a question of minimizing in any way the value of the Socratic method, nor the primary importance of the vital dynamism of the learner. On the contrary, isn't the best tribute to pay to the freedom of the child respecting it and allowing to expand? "The plastic and suggestible freedom of the child is harmed and led astray if it is not helped and guided. An education which consisted in making the child responsible for acquiring information about that of which he does not know he is ignorant, an education which only contemplated a blossoming forth of the child's instincts, and which rendered the teacher a tractable and useless attendant, is but a bankruptcy of education and the responsibility of adults toward the youth" (C, 33).

Self-education, of course; but also being educated in order to have the power of educating oneself. In this respect the art of education imitates the art of medicine; it is an *ars cooperativa naturae,* an instrumental art, an art at the service of the person. "Medicine deals with a living being that possesses inner vitality and the internal principle of health. The doctor exerts real causality in healing a sick man, yet, but in a very particular manner: by

---

[31] The recent work of D. HAMELINE and M.-J. DARDELIN, *La liberté d'apprendre, Situation II* (Paris: Les Editions ouvrières, 1977) is very instructive in this regard.

imitating the ways of nature herself in her operations..." (C, 30).[32] In education, it should be the same. "The teacher exercises a real causal power on the mind of the pupil, but in the manner in which a doctor acts to heal his patient; by assisting nature and co-operating with it" (EM, 60).[33]

Surely "the inner seeing power of intelligence, which naturally and from the very start perceives through sense-experience the primary notions on which all knowledge depends, is thereby able to proceed from what it already knows to what it does not yet know" (C, 31). But this internal principle is to a large extent undetermined, and the child, if he couldn't actively share in an acquired culture, if he wasn't educated, would be unable to progress, except very slowly and with immense difficulty, in his personal life, in the conquest of his freedom. "Obviously to reject the continuity produced by the common labour of generations and the transmission of a doctrinal deposit — above all in the very order of understanding and knowledge — is to opt for darkness" (PM, 2).

Therefore both the primary importance of the inner dynamism of the learner and also the necessary, but subsidiary, role of the teacher must be acknowledged in the educational process. The activity of the one who learns and the activity of the one teaching "are both dynamic factors in education, but that the principal agent in education, the primary dynamic factor or propelling force, is the internal vital principle in the one to be educated; the educator or teacher is only the secondary — though a genuinely effective — dynamic factor and a ministerial agent" (C, 31).

In fact, the role of the teacher is secondary. It is for this reason that "any education which considers the teacher as the principal agent perverts the very nature of the educational task" (C, 32). Maritain confers the hardly flattering name of "education by the rod" on this perversion of education, and he calls it "bad education". A despotical education based on constraint, fear and punishment runs the risk of desensitizing the heart, what is within man; then "there appears a mask, that of the conventional man or that of the rubber-stamped conscience 'incorporated' " (C, 35).

Maritain's position is situated between two extremes. On one hand, he judges the "anarchic" conception of education, which refuses to recognize the necessary role of the teacher and which, as a consequence, risks reducing education to the mere liberation of individuality, as clearly insufficient. "Such educators mistakenly believe they are providing man with the freedom

---

[32] "But when the order of the powers of the human soul is reached, a certain original indetermination by which they find themselves able to take quite different directions is found in all those who participate, even at a distance, in a very decisive way; in order to attain to a true perfection of active potency, they need to gradually emerge from this primary potentiality, from this indetermination; they need culture." M.M. LABOURDETTE, O.P., "Connaissance pratique et savoir moral", in *Jacques Maritain, Son oeuvre philosophique, Revue thomiste*, 1948, p. 146.

[33] "Education, like medicine, is an art cooperating with nature, and the teacher does not cause science to be in the disciple by fashioning him as a sculptor fashions stone or clay, but by putting himself at the service of the active and vital principle which is within the disciple, and which is the principal agent in the acquisition of knowledge, a truth which was already pointed out in *Emile* with some admixtures..." (RI, 308).

of expansion and autonomy to which personality aspires while at the same time they deny the value of all discipline and asceticism, as well as the necessity of striving toward self-perfection" (C, 35). Then, "the ego is in reality scattered among cheap desires or overwhelming passions, and finally submitted to the determinism of matter" (C, 34). On the other hand, he judges as excessive the "despotic conception of education, according to which the primary agent of education would be, not the dynamism of the learner, but rather the teacher who, like a sculptor, would try to impose in a despotic manner the form that he has conceived for him on the mind of the learner. "Such a conception was not infrequent in the education of old. It is a coarse and disastrous conception, contrary to the nature of things. For if the one who is being taught is not an angel, neither is he inanimate clay" (C, 30).

According to Maritain, a middle way should be followed and an efficacious role in education acknowledged for the learner and the teacher: a primary role for the learner since education is related formally to his inner dynamism, located in the order of immanent activity; a necessary, but secondary, role to the educator because he possesses, at least in principle and from the point of view from which he is educating, a knowledge which the learner does not yet have, a human development at which the learner has not yet arrived, an autonomy which the learner must conquer. "His duty is not to mold the child arbitrarily as the potter molds the lifeless clay; rather is his task to assist the mind, the living, spiritual being, which he is endeavoring to develop, and which in that process of development must be the principal agent. For education, like life, is, in the words of philosophy, an immanent activity."[34]

"The education of man is a human awakening" (C, 9). If, as we have explained in chapter II, the conquest of internal freedom and of social freedoms is the response of the person to an appeal to self-overcoming (to autonomy and to independence), the role of the teacher is found on the side of this appeal. That is why, in the first place, he does not have a training role,[35] he has the role of an awakener, "a perpetual appeal to intelligence and free will in the young". In the next chapter, we shall analyze this role of the teacher in its principal components. Briefly, let us say that the true teacher is the one who has "a respect for the soul as well as for the body of the child, the sense of his innermost essence and his internal resources, and a sort of sacred and loving attention to his mysterious identity, which is a hidden thing that no techniques can reach" (C, 9). This basic attitude of the educator — presupposing that he has a personal inner life (EM, 59) and a deep love for the human person — allows for the humanization of education at every stage and in every sphere of activity.

Conceived in this way, the educational task of the adult does not consist in imposing a model to be copied, any more than it means capriciousness and

---

[34] Preface to French Edition in Franz DE HOVRE, *Philosophy and Education*, p. XI.

[35] "I should like to observe now that a kind of animal training, which deals with psychophysical habits, conditioned reflexes, sense-memorization, etc., undoubdtedly plays its part in education: it refers to material individuality, or to what is not specifically human in man. But education is not animal training" (C, 9).

the emancipation from any rule. It consists in guiding the child in his becoming human, requiring of educators "first love and, then, authority — I mean genuine authority, not arbitrary power — intellectual authority to teach and moral authority to be respected and listened to. For the child is entitled to expect from them what he needs: to be positively guided and to learn what he does not know" (EM, 58).

Self-education or education by another: the dilemma does not exist for Maritain. The human being, having to conquer his freedom, not his freedom of choice but his freedom of perfection and of expansion, beginning with innate personal powers that he only possesses originally in a rudimentary and undetermined way, has need of the assistance of educators and first of all of those who have given him his "personal being". And the entire art of education consists in fostering the growth of his personality in the human individual, for the conquest of freedom is, at the same time, the conquest of personality. "The entire art consists in inspiring, schooling and pruning, teaching and enlightening, so that in the intimacy of man's activities the weight of the egoistic tendencies diminishes, and the weight of the aspirations proper to personality and its spiritual generosity increases" (C, 35).

Such is "the duty of the adult to the freedom of the youth" (C, 33).

Chapter IV

Education: A Human Awakening

"In educational matters, as in all matters dealing with man's life, what is of chief importance is the direction of the process, and the implied hierarchy of values" (EM, 44-45).

The education of man is not the mere spontaneous unfolding of natural powers in the direction of material individuality; anymore than it is a kind of training of the human being which would make no appeal to the vital energies of the person. Education is a *human awakening,* a process of integral and integrated development of the person, achieved in the perspective of the conquest of his autonomy, of his freedom. "This internal selfhood grows in proportion as the life of reason and freedom dominates over the life of instinct and sensual desire — which implies self-sacrifice, striving toward self-perfection and love" (C, 34).[1]

In order to realize this difficult progress toward personal expansion, the assistance of educators is required — whose authority is "nothing else than the duty of the adult to the freedom of the youth" (C, 33). For "to achieve rationality and freedom this being must have knowledge taught and discipline, and these require the office of the teacher" (C, 36).

Certainly, the influence of adults on children does not occur without risks — risks, moreover, which are inherent in everything human —; first of all the risk of the domination of grown-ups over the young, either because of "the possessive love" of the parents, or because of the servitude inherent in more or less totalitarian states; the risk, as well, of the irresponsibility and of the absenteeism of adults for whom education consists in giving young people a freedom to do as they please — without distinguishing between capriciousness and autonomy (EM, 59).

---

[1] "When he first sees the light man is only a vague hope. He exists but in germ, and must come to his full development of himself...

"Man is thus called to *enrich himself* in body and in spirit by every kind of cultural activity, and by gradually establishing his dominion over the world; to *possess himself* by way of an infinitely more intimate activity of mind and will, leading to full self-awareness and self-mastery; and to *give himself* in an unforced generosity which shall carry him over his own frontiers and introduce him to the blessed world of communion and love. This call, and the energies it calls forth, commands the structure of the human being, constitutes his abiding worth, and defines the radical law of his action." Jean MOUROUX, *The Meaning of Man* (London: Sheed and Ward, 1948), pp. 130-131.

Maritain conceives the role of adults — of parents and teachers — not as a despotic imposition nor as a "negative education,"[2] but rather as a positive influence completely focused on the spiritual energies of the child. "The educational venture is a ceaseless appeal to intelligence and free will in the young person" (EM, 61).

In his texts on the philosophy of education, Maritain hardly hesitates proposing the means which should be put into operation to achieve the ends of education. It pertains especially to the sciences of education to accomplish this important task and to enrich the pedagogical patrimony with their discoveries. Nevertheless, the philosophy of education has an irreplaceable function to exercise in this realm, namely, that of indicating, starting with the permanent values of the human person (and the aims of education), the direction and the fundamental requirements of the educational process as well as the appropriate role of each educational agent, especially that of the family and the school.

I.- THE DIRECTION AND BASIC REQUIREMENTS OF THE EDUCATION PROCESS

In the chapter devoted to the dynamics of education (C, 29-57), Maritain deals with this question in two stages. First, he enumerates the basic dispositions of human nature to which the educator must pay attention, that is: the love of truth, the love of the good and of justice, simplicity and openness in regard to existence, the sense of a job well done and the spirit of cooperation. Maritain does not pretend to give a complete enumeration here. It can easily be established that these dispositions are connected to the person as such and are related as much to his inner life as they are to his social life. They constitute "the very basis of the task of education" (C, 36); they are like the foundations on which the personality of the learner, or — to use Plato's expression — "the keel of the ship of his existence"[3] will be laid.

In order to foster the blooming and development of these natural dispositions which must be cultivated with care, Maritain shows, in a second stage, "the fundamental rules of education for the teacher or the ministerial agent" (C, 39). These educational norms are as follows: to encourage, to be concerned above all with inwardness, to nourish the internal unity of the person, to liberate the mind by the mastery of reason over the things learned.

It seems to us that these multiple elements of the dynamics of education follow a double curve: a curve which could be designated *existential* and which is related to the attitude held in the face of life, work, and other people;

---

[2]   In this regard, Maritain's position is far from that proposed by Rousseau for the child up to twelve years of age: "Therefore the education of the earliest years should be merely negative. It consists, not in teaching virtue or truth, but in preserving the heart from vice and from the spirit of error. If only you could let well alone, and get others to follow your example; if you could bring your scholar to the age of twelve strong and healthy, but unable to tell his right hand from his left, the eyes of his understanding would be open to reason as soon as you began to teach him. Free from prejudice and free from habits, there would be nothing in him to counteract the effects of your labours." Jean-Jacques ROUSSEAU, *Emile* (New York: J.M. Dent, 1930), pp. 57-58.

[3]   See *Laws*, VII, 803 a and b.

a curve which could be called *sapiential* and which is situated in the development of mind starting with the natural love of truth and ascending to the aspirations after wisdom. This corresponds to the two poles of the human person in his internal life, that is, the cognitive pole (the intellect whose proprer object is being and which is the root of freedom) and the affective pole (the free will whose proper act is love and which is the origin of choices relating to the personal and inter-personal life).

Certainly it is difficult in the concrete process of personal development to disassociate these two aims and their manifold components, since the intellect and the will, although distinct by nature, mutually penetrate each other in the progress of personal life; but we believe that this way of presenting Maritain's thought will allow us to grasp better how education as a human awakening must take into account in a vital way these two internal dynamisms of the person.

A. THE EXISTENTIAL CURVE OR PERSONAL AWAKENING TO THE VALUES OF LIFE: EXISTENCE, WORK, OTHER PERSONS

In this regard, the entire educational process is based on a natural disposition "so elemental", that is simplicity and openness with regard to existence. This disposition is rooted in the very reality of existing: it is good to exist — *ens et bonum convertuntur* — it is a fundamental law of being, the law of "the fecundity of being" (EE, 43).

This fundamental law transposed to the level of the person, when it is not opposed by egotism, pride, unfortunate frustrations, is expressed by "the attitude of a being who exists gladly, is unashamed of existing, stands upright in existence, and for whom to be and to accept the natural limitations of existence are matters of equally simple assent" (C, 37).[4]

This attitude results from the awareness — though confused — of the greatness of the fact of being and of living, from the awareness that this life and its possibilities are gifts. Being is to be loved as well as to love. It is therefore in the knowledge and the recognition of his subjective being that the person discovers "the basic generosity of existence. Subjectivity, this essentially dynamic, living and open centre, both receives and gives. It receives through the intellect, by superexisting in knowledge. It gives through the will, by superexisting in love: that is, by having within itself other beings as inner attractions toward them and toward giving oneself to them, and by spiritually existing in the manner of a gift" (RR, 91-92).

Unfortunately, it would seem that our contemporary society, though crammed with material goods — and maybe somehow because of that — has

---

[4] In *Carnet de notes* (p. 21), Maritain, referring back to his old memories of 1901-1902, gives a very fine description of this attitude as personally experienced. "If life was really understood, it would be seen that it is necessary to take what happens each day as a 'grace' dispensed from day to day: the evil as well as the good; perhaps especially the good. It is wonderful that such joy happened to me. Life owes me nothing. No one owes me anything."

great difficulties in nourishing this basic attitude so very important for human progress. All kinds of social disorders, negative attitudes toward life (the crumbling of the family, abortion, drug abuse, suicides, psychological instability etc.) appear as so many symptoms of a sick society in which the feeling of insecurity spreads, and in which it seems more and more difficult for the human child — as he grows and discovers what is going on around him — to willingly exist, to be grateful and happy to be alive. Now "fear and trembling... are bad beginnings in education" (C, 38).

Nevertheless, a positive attitude in the face of existence is required for the harmonious development of the person; it is the natural ground, the humus of the human virtues of magnanimity and humility, it is the basis of the joy of existing. And education, the personal meaning of the educational endeavour is of crucial important in this regard. To educate, in its most profound sense, is not only to act on behalf of someone, to be of service to them; it is first and foremost "to exist with",[5] a *co-existence* which is love, a reception given to the person, an attention paid to him. It is in such an educational atmosphere that the child can awaken to what is human. And it is why the family, which constitutes "the primary educational sphere", is so important for the blossoming of the child's personality.

"The most precious gift of an educator is a sort of sacred and loving attention to the child's mysterious identity, which is a hidden thing that no techniques can reach. Encouragement is as fundamentally necessary as humiliation is harmful" (EM, 61). In order to foster the awakening of the person and stimulate an expansive impetus, this loving attention must comprise two features which cannot be dissociated: it must be directed toward the spiritual preconscious (inwardness) and it should be expressed in the form of encouragement.

The genuine educator has as a basic rule "to center attention on the inner depths of personality and its preconscious spiritual dynamism, in other words,

---

[5]   "Whenever we have to deal with the ingredients of human history, we are prone to consider matters from the point of view of *action* or of the *ideas* which shape action. Yet it is necessary to consider them also — and primarily — from the point of view of existence. I mean that there is another, and more fundamental, order than that of social and political action: it is the order of communion in life, desire and suffering. In other words there must be recognized, as distinct from the category of *to act for* or *to act with*, the category *to exist with* and *to suffer with* which concerns a more profound order of reality.

"*To act for* belongs to the realm of mere benevolence. *To exist with* and *to suffer with* to the realm of love in unity. Love is given to an existing, concrete being. Despite what Pascal says, one loves persons, not 'qualities'. The one I love, I love him, right or wrong; and I wish to exist with him and suffer with him.

"*To exist with* is an ethical category. It does not mean to live with someone in a physical sense, or in the same way as he lives; it means loving someone in the sense of becoming one with him, of bearing his burdens, of living a common moral life with him, of feeling with him and suffering with him.

"If one loves that human and living thing which is called 'the people', and which, like all human and living things is, I know, very difficult to define, but all the more real, then one's first and basic wish will be to exist with the people, to suffer with the people, and to stay in communion with the people." *The Range of Reason*, p. 121.

to lay stress on inwardness and the internalization of the influence'' (C, 39). That means, then, the educational act cannot be satisfied just to touch lightly the intellect and the will of the child by presenting to it ready-made knowledge — made by and for adults, but miniaturized for the sake of those younger — by stimulating its action uniquely by extraneous factors like personal interest, competition and so forth (C, 40). Such a way of operating runs the risk of leaving the vital energies of the child dormant. An appeal should be made to the "sources of knowledge and poetry, of love and truly human desires, hidden in the spiritual darkness of the intimate vitality of the soul'' (C, 41), which requires a personal contact between the educator and the learner, "but above all to give to that mysterious identity of the child's soul, which is unknown to himself, and which no techniques can reach, the comforting assurance of being in some way recognized by a human personal gaze, inexpressible either in concepts or words'' (C, 41).

This attention to the inwardness of the learner must be exercised in an atmosphere of encouragement, even if sometimes it may appear necessary to use repression, provided that this "repression of bad tendencies will always be bound up with enlightenment and encouragement'' (C, 39). It can rightly be said that encouragement is like the sun of the soul's culture; it is through encouragement that education can become a liberation. "To liberate the good energies is the best way of repressing the bad ones'' and "encouragement is as fundamentally necessary as humiliation is harmful'' (C, 39).[6]

Thanks to the attention paid to the inner riches still unexploited and not even consciously perceived, and thanks to the encouragement which is both a recognition of the resources of the child and an incentive for developing these resources, the natural disposition of the child to "exist gladly'' will have the opportunities of transforming itself, at the level of the conscious life, into a joy grateful to exist, in a dynamic assumption of personal talents and in an active will to make them bear fruit.

In short, if it is desired that children, old and young, be unashamed of existing and stand upright in existence, by assuming existence with a deep enthusiasm unceasingly renewed (with magnanimity and humility) — and this through the hardships and risks which are inherent in existence — it is imperative to make them mindful of their own resources and of their own potentialities for the beauty of well-doing (C, 39).

For the child, the fact of being recognized by "a human personal gaze'' will surely nourish his positive attitude toward existing gladly; it will stimulate his natural feeling "of faithfulness and responsibility'' toward his work. And this is so important, "for next to the attitude toward existence there is nothing more basic in man's psychic life than the attitude toward work'' (C, 38). According to Maritain, this probity in regard to work "which is the first natural move toward self-discipline'' is "an essential basis of human morality'' (C, 38).

---

[6] Do we not find here a golden rule which should inspire teachers in school evaluations?

The respect for a work to be achieved, the sense of a job well done, shows respect and love for what is human; is not work a human activity born in the heart of the person and in some way his expression? Respect for himself is expressed in respect for his work. He expresses in it as well the feeling for others, for work is not only self-expression, it is also in the service of others.[7] That is why the love of existence becomes in concrete terms the love of the work well done and the educator must foster both kinds of love himself. Here again, there is a reciprocal causal influence. Of poets, philosophers, artists and scientists, Maritain has written: "But if love does not set them to the work, the chances are that the work will be mediocre or merely futile" (T, 11). This assertion could just as well be applied to learners (and to educators) and then means that if love does not set them to the work, the chances are their existence will be mediocre or merely futile.

An educational environment mindful of persons and of their inner resources will foster the blossoming of a positive attitude toward life and toward work; it will also allow by encouragement — the sign of true love — the sense of the good and justice as well as that of cooperation to bloom. For it is natural for human beings to love the good and justice; it is likewise natural for them to want to live with their fellow-men and along with them to build the good life of the community in friendship and fraternity. The good is the proper object of the will and the sense of justice is a spontaneous quality in children. This love of the good and of justice is, along with the love of the job well done, the basis of moral and social education; starting from this irreplaceable basis, the educator must foster "the love of heroic facts" (C, 37) while remembering that "the saints and the martyrs are the true educators of mankind" (C, 25).[8]

B. The Sapiential Curve or the Love of Truth
directed toward Wisdom

Human existence can only express itself in its personal and social dimensions by way of the intellect. And the education of the person cannot be reduced to a kind of affective bursting forth from which any preoccupation with the life of the mind would be absent.

When an impersonal and anonymous atmosphere exists, there is a great temptation to overestimate the values of feeling to the detriment of those of the intellect. Still what would human affectivity not rooted in the intellect and unpermeated with awareness be?

In relation to the life of the mind — and as might be expected — Maritain mentions "the love of truth, which is the primary tendency of any intellectual nature" (C, 36),[9] as the first disposition to foster in the child. At

---

[7]   See above, p. 45.

[8]   "What Bergson also saw quite clearly is that there is no entirely right moral life without that aspiration (it may be more or less unconscious, and more lived than known) which he held to be awakened in the human race by the call of the heroes and saints and which is aspiration to the perfection of love." Jacques MARITAIN, *Moral Philosophy* (New York: Charles Scribner's Sons, 1964), p. 435.

[9]   "The ideas of truth, freedom, and man are so closely bound up with one another that we must grasp their interrelationships if we are to achieve a right understanding of the education of man." D. and I. GALLAGHER, in the introduction to *The Education of Man*, p. 10.

issue is an immediate corollary of his conception of the human intellect and of the person. The love of truth is a natural and very precious quality of the intellect; it must be cultivated with a great deal of attention in our day when the communications media try to put the mind to sleep by replacing the true with the "useful", by replacing the intellect with an appeal to the irrational appetites — greatly risking dulling the sense of truth rather than awakening it. "The faculty of language has been so dishonored, the meaning of words so thoroughly falsified; so many truths, met with at every corner in press or radio reports, are at each moment so perfectly mixed with so many errors similarly advertized, and trumpeted to the skies, that men are simply losing the sense of truth" (RR, 116-117).

Yet "by being concerned for truth, and by grasping it, the spirit transcends time" (PG, 14) and frees itself. "The intellect tends to grasp and conquer being" (EM, 47), and this progressive conquest is its life and joy. That is why a truly human education must foster the love of truth, equip the mind of the learner for truth by making him capable "of judging according to the worth of evidence, of enjoying truth and beauty for their own sake, and of advancing, when he has become a man, toward wisdom and some understanding of those things which bring to him intimations of immortality" (EM, 48).

To this end, it is necessary to be constantly vigilant to respect the mind's stages of development "in order to awaken progressively the child and the youth to seek and perceive truth for the sake of truth, to exercise their power to think, and to sense the joy of intellection" (EM, 56). So then, the intellect can expand itself in the joy of knowing and direct itself toward wisdom, by basing itself on the natural love of truth, whose outward signs are wonder and amazement. Moreover, the search for truth is neither easy, nor hopeless; it does require reflection and effort.[10]

For this reason the assistance of the educator is so precious here, and, for it to be positive and efficacious, this assistance should fix its attention on the liberation of *the power of intuition, should tend to unify not to scatter,* so as to make sure that the student's reason *truly masters the things learned.*

We cannot insist too much on the primary role of the teacher in regard to the intellectual awakening of the child, that is the freeing of the intuitive power. The human mind naturally aspires to truth; we must not sacrifice this aspiration toward the joy of knowing "to cramming memorization or to conventional rules of skill in making use of concepts or words" (C, 42). What matters over and above everything else is "the awakening of the inner resources and creativity" (C, 43), intellectual insight and intuition.

At this point, the multiplication of material facilities and educational means is of little use; what especially counts is to pay attention to the inner

---

[10] "You will agree that man, by the very fact that he is a rational animal — the most perfect of animals and the least perfect of spirits — is a being in whom the intellect exercises its primacy only with difficulty and with many an eclipse and that an all too natural slope leads him to search for easy ideas, to economize thought, to judge according to what he wants and not according to what is — in short to cripple the intellectual life within him." *Theonas,* p. 59.

core of intellectual vitality, the intuitive power of the learner. And how? "By moving forward along the paths of spontaneous interest and natural curiosity, by grounding the exercise of memory in intelligence, and primarily by giving courage, by listening a great deal, and by causing the youth to trust and give expression to those spontaneous poetic or noetic impulses of his own" (C, 43). In order to do this, the educator must know how to listen and stimulate the spontaneous expression of the wakening mind; he must respect the natural path of spiritual awakening, that is sense perception, sense experience and imagination;[11] and above all, he should never disappoint the thirst for "seeing" which dwells in the young intellect, a thirst which is "a tendency toward an object to be grasped. And to the extent that this tendency is set free, and the intellect becomes accustomed to grasping, seeing, expressing the objects toward which it tends, to that very extent its intuitive power is liberated and strengthened" (C, 44).[12]

The art of the teacher consists in imitating the ways the intellectual nature follows in its own operations. "Thus the teacher has to offer to the mind either examples from experience or particular statements which the pupil is able to judge by virtue of what he already knows and from which he will go on to discover broader horizons" (C, 31). This obviously presupposes that the teacher is himself concerned with discerning and seeing, with having the vision and understanding of that which is. "There is no knowledge without intuitivity."[13] Intuitivity must pervade all his teaching. It is the necessary condition so that he may be able "to center the acquisition of knowledge and solid formation of the mind on the freeing of the learner's intuitive power" (EM, 61). In this way, he will constantly keep the mind of the pupil alert which accordingly will become more and more eager to know and which will aspire more or less consciously for wisdom.

The teacher concerned with freeing the minds of his pupils or students, moreover, must be vigilant that he does not dissipate their energies in vain curiosity, and must look to satisfy "the essential need and aspiration of the mind to be freed in unity" (C, 47). This need is inscribed in the very nature of

---

[11] Maritain's pedagogical advice recalls that of Jean-Jacques Rousseau relating to the necessity of "cultivating the senses" (see *Emile,* pages 97-116 in the Foxley translation, published by J.M. Dent).

[12] "Before giving a youth the rules of good style, let us tell him first never to write anything which does not seem to him really beautiful, whatever the result may be. In the first approach to mathematics, physics, or philosophy, let us see to it that the student actually grasps each step of the simplest mathematical demonstration, however slow this may be — that he actually understands in the laboratory how logically the statement of the physicist emerges from the experiment — that he becomes intensely involved, through the very anxiety of his mind, in the first great philosophical problems, and after that, that he really sees the solution. In asking a youth to read a book, let us get him to undertake a real spiritual adventure and meet and struggle with the internal world of a given man, instead of glancing over a collection of bits of thought and dead opinions, looked upon from without and with sheer indifference, according to the horrible custom of so many victims of what they call 'being informed'. Perhaps with such methods the curriculum will lose a little in scope which will be all to the good" (C, 44-45).

[13] Such is the title of an article by Maritain published in the *Revue Thomiste* in 1970 (pp. 30-71).

the mind whose natural development calls for wisdom[14] the acme of this development which can only be approached in unity. Like the human person, human knowledge can only tend toward its perfection by the ways of unity.[15] Maritain suggests three ways of nourishing internal unity in man: manual labour, the union of reason and experience, the unity of aspiration and vision.

The human intellect is not the intellect of a pure spirit; it is located in a being composed of mind and matter. The importance of developing the mind in a symbiotic relation with the body comes from this as does the importance of manual labour which, according to Maritain, ought to accompany the education of the mind until the end of secondary school (or pre-University education). "There is no place closer to man than a workshop, and the intelligence of a man is not only in his head, but in his fingers too. Not only does manual work further psychological equilibrium, but it also furthers ingenuity and accuracy of the mind, and is the prime basis of artistic activity" (C, 45). The pedagogical value of manual work should be stressed all the more since in the world of tomorrow the dignity of work will probably be more clearly recognized.

The development of the intellect in the direction of unity also requires that a vital link be established between experience and reason, for "education and teaching must start with experience, but in order to complete themselves with reason"; such is the condition of the intellect of a *rational animal.* In opposition to empiricism which exploits experience to the detriment of the highest functions of reason, experience must be taught to realize itself in rational knowledge; and contrary to rationalism which scorns experience, reason must be taught to base itself on experience. "Education must inspire eagerness both for experience and for reason" (C, 46), and help uncover their reciprocal connections.

Finally, the educator must insist on the organic unity of knowledge. His teaching must be permeated with a "vision of wisdom", a vision all the more important and necessary since contemporary culture offers to the young intelligence a great array of knowledge (product of the progress made in science) and contemporary society tends to functionalize human life and dissipate it. "If a man does not over-come the inner multiplicity of his drives

---

[14]   "That knowledge we call wisdom, which penetrates and embraces things with the deepest, most universal, and most united insights. Such a knowledge, which lives not only by supreme science, but also by human and spiritual experience, is over and above any field of specialization, for it has to do with realities which permeate each and every being and with aspirations which call to the very nature and freedom of man. It is in itself the highest value for the human mind (C, 48).

[15]   The person "if he would make a success of himself..has to maintain his coherence through all the risks that time may bring. This demands a permanent integration of all the elements corporeal, psychical, social, spiritual, which are given and needed from time to time." Jean MOUROUX, *The Meaning of Man* (London: Sheed and Ward, 1948), pp. 132-133.

"If there are permanent traits in the human psyche, perhaps the most prominent are man's rejection of agonizing contradictions, his intolerance of excessive tension, the individual's striving for intellectual consistency, his search for happiness identified not with the mechanical satisfaction of appetite but with the concrete realization of his potentialities and with his idea of himself as one reconciled to his fate — that of the complete man." Edgar FAURE and others, *Learning to Be* (Paris: Unesco; London: Harrap, 1972), p. 154.

and especially of the diverse currents of knowledge and belief and the diverse vital energies at play in his mind, he will always remain more a slave than a free man'' (C, 47). Education should then be inspired by the feeling for unity, the spirit of universality, that is, by ''a universal and articulate comprehension of human achievements in science and culture'', adapted to the several levels of the development of the mind.[16]

From this standpoint, the compartmentalization of university specialization must be considered as a great weakness just as the premature specialization of secondary education whose courses are sometimes offered as miniature university ones.

To guide education in the direction of unity and of universality ''presupposes that the mind of the adults, especially the teachers', is not itself in a state of division and anarchy, and that the adults are in possession of what they have to communicate, namely, wisdom and integrated knowledge'' (EM, 59). Only those teachers directed toward wisdom will be able to respond to the ''essential need and aspiration of the mind to be freed in unity'' (C, 47).

It is worthwhile recalling ''that there is no unity or integration without a stable hierarchy of values'' and that ''knowledge and love of what is above time are superior to, and embrace and quicken, knowledge and love of what is within time'' (EM, 53).[17] In this regard, Maritain notes sadly that contemporary education all too often frustrates the most vital needs of the mind. ''It is a pity to see so many young people bewildered by highly developed and specialized, but chaotic, instruction about anything whatever in the field of particular sciences and miserably ignorant of everything that concerns God and the deepest realities in man and the world'' (EM, 55).

In addition to intuitivity and the sense of unity, there is a third quality essential for the development of the intellect, namely ''the mastery of reason over the things learned'' (C, 49). It is not just useless but harmful to burden the mind of the pupil with a growing amount of ''knowledge'', if it is not assured that he has really understood through an active and vital assimilation. Learning is understanding. ''What is learned should never be passively or mechanically received, as dead information which weighs down and dulls the mind. It must rather be actively transformed by understanding into the very life of the mind, and thus strengthen the latter, as wood thrown into fire and transformed into flame makes the fire stronger'' (C, 50).[18]

---

[16] ''The universality adapted to the young readers of fairy tales and *Alice in Wonderland* is of quite another nature than that fitted to the students reading Kant or Spinoza'' (C, 49).

[17] The pedagogical order does not necessarily follow the order of values. See *The Education of Man*, p. 56.

[18] ''In the first place, we will bring our attention to bear on what it is to learn to swim, to dance, etc.; here to learn will be to make oneself capable of exercising some activity, and it is quite clear that that is to free onself to some extent, even if afterwards, what has been at first a liberation may run the risk, through lack of certain precautions, of becoming a form of slavery.

''But, above all, we will have to remind ourselves that learning is nothing, if it is not to some degree, understanding, and the intellectualists of all ages, from Plato to Spinoza, have never ceased bringing to light the fact, undeniable in my opinion, that understanding is essentially freeing oneself.'' Gabriel MARCEL, ''La liberté en 1971'' in *Les Etudes philosophiques,* January-March, 1975, page 15.

According to a certain stylish vocabulary, we would say that one should foster the blossoming of a *critical mind* in the student.

However, education of the critical mind should not be confused with a mere dialectics of the mind from which the very soul of education would be missing, that is, the striving to understand, the impetus toward knowledge. According to Maritain, that is why "to raise clever doubts, to prefer searching to finding, and perpetually to pose problems without ever solving them are the great enemies of education" (C, 50). Maritain is not against the way of interrogation, the socratic method in education, far from it. "If we pass now to the question of learning by way of solving problems, I would say that this method of learning is normally a way to truth-grasping or contemplative learning, just as *praxis* is a way to knowledge" (EM, 57). By means of this, education is prevented from degenerating into passivity and inert docility; the initiative of the learner is upheld.

There is no duty more primordial than that of maintaining vigilance over "what corresponds to the primary aim of education, that is, both truth to be known at the various degrees of the scale of knowledge and the capacity to think and make a personal judgement, to be developed, equipped, and firmly established" (EM, 58). For the freeing of the mind of the learner cannot be achieved by a mere gymnastic exercise of its powers. "It is by truth that it is set free, when truth is really known, that is, vitally assimilated by the insatiable activity which is rooted in the depths of self" (C, 52). Which doesn't mean that the educator imposes "his truths" on the learner. But he himself must live in conformity with the law of the mind and according to the pedagogical principle derived from it. That is why "the first duty of a teacher is to develop within himself, for the sake of truth, deeprooted convictions, and frankly to manifest them, while taking pleasure, of course, in having the student develop, possibly against them, his own personal convictions" (EM, 138).

If the pure gymnastics of the mind does not have any great educational value by itself, the passive reception of knowledge (or of the educator's opinions), the servility of the mind, are equally opposed to the fundamental requirements of a genuine education and the life of the mind.

Intellectual formation is both a noble and a delicate endeavour; it can only be achieved in an absolute respect for the personal inwardness of the learner and by constant encouragement to develop the basic qualities of the intellect in its gradual advances toward the truth, that is, intuitivity, the sense of unity and the critical sense. This is the direction that any education worthy of the name and hopeful of fostering the natural growth of the human mind must take. Such is the profound meaning of what Maritain calls *a liberal education*, that education which prepares the youth "to exercise his power to think in a genuinely free and liberating manner — that is to say, when it equips him for truth and makes him capable of judging according to the worth of evidence, of enjoying truth and beauty for their own sake, and of advancing when he has become a man, toward wisdom and some understanding of those things which bring to him intimation of immortality" (EM, 48).

II.- EDUCATIONAL INFLUENCES

An education for freedom, able to foster the integral and integrated development of the person, centred on the conquest of inner or spiritual freedom, and extending itself in the apprenticeship of social freedoms and social responsibilities, requires the positive action of educators; these educators will allow the learner to share in a dynamic way in cultural achievements, which are not inherited at birth, and will assist him in directing himself toward an ever deepening educational autonomy.

This positive influence of the educator, if it is to be beneficial must be located in the very movement of the personal dynamics of the learner, and therefore must be quite attentive to his inner resources; this positive influence must strengthen especially the personal dispositions of the learner in regard to existence, truth, the good, work, other persons. It must help him to grow "in age and wisdom".

But who are these educators and what role can each of them play towards the growing human being? In this regard, Maritain treats particularly the specific role of the family and of the school as "educational spheres",[19] all the while recognizing that the school of life has a determining influence on education.

A. THE FAMILY

The family is "the first and fundamental educational sphere, grounded in nature". The proper role of the family is found in the realm of moral education.[20] It is both the privilege and the great responsiblity of the family to foster the blossoming of the moral life in children. "What does a great deal for virtue is love" (C, 95),[21] and love regards existing persons. The family is the primary natural environment in which this love can take shape, express itself and grow. "Is not family love the primary pattern of any love uniting a community of men? Is not fraternal love the very name of the neighborly love which is but one with the love of God?" (C, 96).

In spite of the serious difficulties through which the contemporary family is passing, in spite of the many assaults which it undergoes by reason of current economic and social conditions, "the nature of things cannot be changed. And it is in the nature of things that the vitality and virtues of love develop first in the family" (C, 96).

All too often it happens that in the family the child becomes "a victim of psychological traumatisms, or of the bad example, ignorance, or prejudice of

---

[19]   "By educational spheres I mean those collective entities which have always been recognized as especially committed to educational training: namely the family, the school, the state, and the Church" (C, 24).

[20]   "Now the point I would like to insist upon is that, if the first responsibility of the school deals with the intellect and with knowledge, and if the first and direct responsibility for moral education belongs to the family group and the churches, nevertheless the responsibility of the educational system in this regard is, however indirect, no less necessary" (EM, 105).

"According to the nature of things, moral education is more the task of the family, assisted by the religious community to which it belongs, than the task of the school" (EM, 44).

[21]   See, on this issue, *The Education of Man*, pp. 114-117.

the adult" (C, 24), which doesn't mean that one ought to get rid of family life altogether; then the cure would be worse than the disease. The educational work of the family constitutes it as the school "where the feelings and the will of the child are naturally shaped" (C, 97)[22]: parental example, the rules of conduct they inculcate in their children, the inspiration and religious habits they further, the memories of their own lineage they convey, but also common experiences: trials, joys, endeavours, hopes, suffering, "the daily love which grows up in the midst of cuffs and kisses" (C, 97), experiences of everyday life (which is the best kind of sexual education) are this school.

For the child, then, "the society made up by his parents, his brothers, and sisters, is the primary human society and human environment in which, consciously and subconsciously, he becomes acquainted with love and from which he receives his ethical nourishment" (C, 97).[23]

B. THE SCHOOL

The education received in the family needs to be completed by school education whose proper task — at once necessary and partial — is teaching.

It is illusory to hope that the school assume the total responsibility for the education of youth and believe that the young man, upon leaving the school or the University, will have completed his education. "It must be observed", Maritain says, "that education, in the broad sense of the word, continues during the entire lifetime of every one of us. The school system is only a *partial* and *inchoative* agency with respect to the tasks of education. Moreover, because it deals essentially with that which can be taught, it refers to the education and formation of intelligence more than of the will" (EM, 51).

Our education is a process which lasts a lifetime; in this regard, then, the school has only a preparatory role,[24] and a partial role, concerning before anything else knowledge and the intellect.[25] The proper domain of school education — of teaching — is *truth*. "The only dominating influence in the school and the college must be that of truth" (C, 26).

---

[22] That is indeed the role that Alain recognizes for the family: "Surely the family group with the children and grown-ups together, and that natural distribution of powers and duties is something beautiful and that nothing can replace; here is the school of feeling; here devotion, trust, admiration come into play; the boys imitate the father, and the girls imitate the mother, each being both protector and protected, venerated and venerating." ALAIN, *Propos sur l'éducation* (Paris: P.U.F, 15th edition, 1972), p. 22.

[23] Moral education is also the responsibility of the Church. "It is not my purpose to speak now of the other educational sphere directly concerned with the moral shaping of man, namely the Church, acting by means of its teaching, precepts, sacrements, and liturgy, and its spiritual training and guidance, as well as by its manifold initiatives and undertakings, youth movements and organizations. Suffice it to say that here again we are confronted with the law of love proper to the family, this time the very family of God... (EM, 120).

[24] "We have already noted that the teaching of the school and the university is a preparation for an education of and by himself that man pursues all his life long" (PE, 169-170).

[25] "School and college education has indeed its own world, which essentially consists of the dignity and achievements of knowledge and the intellect, that is, of the human being's root faculty. And of this world itself that knowledge which is wisdom is the ultimate goal" (C, 28).

In no way does this mean that the school should not concern itself with other aspects of education, especially moral and social education. For the part — teaching — is not to be separated from the whole. The business of the school is not with pure intellects, but with concrete persons; therefore, in carrying out its specific task, it should respect the wholeness of man and of his education. "Any teaching worthy of the name is permeated with educational values and, as a result, brings into play, at least to some extent and in an indirect way, basic notions, of a philosophical and religious order, the idea of man and his destiny, and the basic inspiration on which the educational operation inevitably depends" (PE, 186).

As to moral formation, the appropriate role of the school is an indirect one and is exercised by way of knowledge, that is to say, by way of moral teaching. "Thus it is chiefly through the instrumentality of intelligence and truth that the school and the college may affect the powers of desire, will, and love in the youth, and help him gain control of his tendential dynamism" (C, 26).

Yet, to the extent that the school is a living environment, a medium of interpersonal relationships, it also exercises — like the family and in an analogous way — a profound and direct influence on the moral and social life of children. From this angle, everything in the school, as in the family, can contribute to educating: the professors' attitudes, school regulations, the sense of freedom, respect for other persons, relations with authority, etc. That is why Maritain recommends that the pupil actively participate in the life of the school. "In a manner adapted to the age and capacity of students, schools and universities should be laboratories in the responsibilities of freedom and the qualities of the mind proper to democratic citizenship" (EM, 68).

But if the school co-operates in this way in the social education of the youth, does this mean that it thus becomes an agent in the service of the state?

First of all it must be remembered that the primary goal of the school, according to Maritain, is not *social;* it is defined in relation to the intellect. First of all, the school should be "helping minds to become articulate, free and autonomous" (EM, 59). The school faithful to its educational ideal is neither a bastion of the established order nor a weapon for the social revolution; it tries very simply — and that is no easy thing — to form citizens aware of their social responsibilities, enlightened citizens with critical minds who will be able to actively involve themselves in social and political life. From this perspective, the role of the school is neither conservative nor revolutionary; it is — or should be — liberating.[26] Moreover, that is the finest service that the school can provide to persons and society; let it realize this in

---

[26] "Education should essentially aim not at producing the type but at liberating the human person" (C, 100).

It appears that Maritain's position resembles that of Paulo Freire, summed up by F.C. Wellfort in the preface to *L'éducation pratique de la liberté* (Paris, Editions du Cerf, 2nd Edition, 1973): "A pedagogy of freedom can help a populistic politics, for the raising of consciousness allows one to understand how social structures are used as instruments of domination and violence; but it pertains to politicians, not to the educator, to guide this awareness in a specifically political direction" (p. 21).

the least imperfect way possible, and it will have earned the esteem of mankind.

Again it is for this reason that the school ought to enjoy the most complete freedom of action in regard to the state, this freedom commonly called academic freedom in America. For the changes in the last few decades have led the state to play an increasingly important role in establishing and financing school systems; the state should play its role while respecting the greatest educational autonomy possible, ''in freedom and for freedom'' (C, 92).

C. THE SCHOOL OF LIFE

''What is most important in education is not the job of education, and still less that of learning'' (C, 22). Everything cannot be taught in the school. Intuition and love, not topics to be taught, are gift and freedom. There are courses in philosophy, there are none in wisdom, nor in happiness. That doesn't mean that the educator should not be concerned with intuition and love, with wisdom and happiness. Quite the contrary, for these realities are at the heart of any human education. For instance, the intellectual foundations of moral life and the virtues can and should be taught, but virtue cannot be taught. Intuition is not taught, but the educator centres his teaching on the intuitivity of knowledge.

In this respect, Maritain acknowledges the privileged importance of the educative influence of ''extra-educational spheres'', that is, the influence of the school of life.[27] The whole field of human activity has an educational value, and its influence can bend the evolution of the person much more deeply than all the lessons learned at school: ''everyday work and pain, hard experiences in friendship and love, social customs, law (which is 'pedagogue', according to Saint Paul), the common wisdom embodied in the behavior of the people, the inspiring radiance of art and poetry, the penetrating influence of religious feasts and liturgy...'' (C, 25).[28]

Finally, Maritain maintains that the supremely important educative factor is ''that call of the hero which Henri Bergson so insistently emphasized, and which passes through the whole structure of social habits and moral regulations as a vitalizing aspiration toward the infinite Love which is the source of being'' (C, 25).[29]

---

[27] It seems that Plato recognized the educational importance of life; as a consequence, in his ideal city, he recommended two years of ''compulsory physical training'' as a means of perfecting the education already received and especially to test the moral worth of future candidates for the class of state guardians. See *The Republic*, VII, 537b.

[28] From the viewpoint of life (in society), the State also has an educational role. ''Doubtless, the State has a moral and not merely material function; the law has an educational function and tends to develop moral virtues...'' (RM, 77). See also *Freedom and the Modern World*, p. 79.

[29] Contemporary youth is sensitive to this call of the hero. That cluster of young people who devote a period of their lives to the service of the poorest in their own country as in foreign lands testifies to it.

Whoever he may be, the learner is therefore influenced by many agents and in many ways in the educational process through which "he forms himself as a man". He will only become a man, that is, an authentic and autonomous human person, insofar as, by virtue of his inner resources, enlightened by truth, animated by the love of the good, he will take charge of his own destiny and will direct himself toward the conquest of his internal and social freedom, in an attitude of openness to existence and in a spirit of communion with men.

However limited and modest the necessary role of the educator may be, it only has the opportunity to become a "human awakening" to the extent that the educator will heed the inner resources of the learner and will fulfill his own role, whether in the family or the school, in such a way that "in the intimacy of man's activities the weight of the egoistic tendencies diminishes, and the weight of the aspirations proper to personality and its spiritual generosity increases" (C, 35). In this way, the learner will be greatly helped to profit more from "the school of life", that is, from the daily experiences which will be like so many influences fostering "the education of and by himself that man pursues all his lifelong".

Chapter V

The School and Liberal Education

In his philosophy of education, Maritain has emphasized the aims of the educational process, namely the freeing of the person first in his inner life, and subsequently in his social life. He has shown how the educational art expresses "the duty of the adult to the freedom of the child"; and then pointed out the direction of the educational process as a human awakening.

We have been able to establish that this "education for freedom" is based on a metaphysics of the person, the latter conceived as a being enjoying "the spiritual superexistence of knowledge and love", as a being thirsting for truth and capable of giving himself "to beings who are as other selves for him".

In the light of this philosophy of education and mindful of the cultural evolution of our societies, Maritain has proposed a very interesting arrangement of academic programs; he has especially concentrated on the curricula of secondary education, without however neglecting the university. He has also tackled the difficult questions of moral education and of religious education in the school environment.

In chapter V, we shall try and uncover the meaning of Maritain's reflections bearing on these questions.

I.- TO EDUCATE OR TO INSTRUCT

A. The Appropriate Role of the School

According to Maritain, it would be an illusion and even non-sensical to ask the school to ensure the complete formation of man. "Our education goes on until our death" (C, 26)[1]. In no way does this mean that school or the university should be attended throughout all one's life. In this regard, the fundamental role of the school "is a preparation for an education of the self by

---

[1] Some fear, wrongly we believe, that lifelong education leads to an unduly protracted schooling.

"There is a risk that the development of lifelong formation in the present setting of national education tends to a kind of total schooling of our society: instead of being in compulsory schooling only from age 6 to 16, workers would be subjected from age 6 to 65 to a school and university apparatus..." J.W. LaPierre, "Un terrain de lutte", in *Esprit*, no. 439, October, 1974, p. 464.

the self that man pursues throughout his lifetime'' (PE, 169-170).[2] Guiding education towards autodidacticism is but the corollary of the ministerial role of the educator in interaction with the inner resources of the learner; it results as well from the need for enlightened and active citizens in a democratic society. ''The education of tomorrow must provide the common man with the means for his personal fulfillment, not only with regard to his labour but also with regard to his social and political activities in the civil commonwealth, and to the activities of his leisure hours'' (C, 90).

Moreover, in the preparatory sphere of self-education, school education has only a partial job — although a very important one — which primarily concerns knowledge and the intellect. Its proper role is to *instruct* and is located on the developmental curve of the mind beginning with the initial love of the truth in its movement toward wisdom: ''according to the nature of things, moral education is more the task of the family, assisted by the religious community to which it belongs, than the task of the school'' (EM, 144).

The primary concern of the school is that of *truth,* that is, the concern for the personal and internalized development of the intellect in the direction of ''the mastery of reason over the things learned'', and for the blossoming of the critical mind. It is the duty of the school ''to keep alive the sense of truth in the student; to regard his intellectual and spiritual aspirations and every beginning in him of creative activity and personal grasping of reality; never, as St. Thomas puts it, to dig a pit before him without filling it up, to appeal to the intuitive power of his mind, and to offer to him a unified and intergrated universe of knowledge'' (EM, 137).

The progress of the learner toward intellectual autonomy, which doesn't exclude action, must be fostered through an atmosphere where silence and personal effort prevail (EM, 56-57). For the educational perspective must be mindful both of the hierarchy of values — which ''demands that practical action on the world and on the human community superabound from contemplation of truth'' (EM, 56), — and the concrete development of the child. A change of perspective may be required ''in order to awaken progressively the child and the youth to seek and perceive truth for the sake of truth, to exercise their power to think, and to sense the joy of intellection. From praxis to knowledge, this is the normal method of education, especially in its first steps'' (EM, 56).

In short, the classroom must foster, in an appropriate atmosphere, the awakening of the power of understanding, and, to this end, the teacher cannot be content with mechanical drills nor with ready-made formulas; he must constantly make an appeal to the thirst for knowledge and to the critical activity of the learner ''whose reward will be the very joy of perceiving truth'' (EM, 58). In order to arrive there, the learner needs to be guided by an inspired teacher, not by that paternalistic attitude which wants to stamp its

---

[2]   See also *The Education of Man,* p. 83. According to Maritain, this basic orientation of the school does not rule out the possibility of recurrent education or of the need for school attendance by those who are already in the labour market (PE, 90).

image on the child, but by love, attentive to the child's inner resources and having the intellectual authority over him in order to teach (and make him learn what he does not know) and the moral authority to make himself respected and listened to.[3]

The primary role of the school is to *instruct,* in order that the learner *learns* and understands, and is progressively directed towards self-education which is an important component of education. There is no opposition between instruction and education. The school educates while instructing; it educates all the more as its teaching is situated in the perspective of a holistic education taking into account the substantial unity of the human being and the laws of his progression.

A human being is neither a mere animal, nor a pure spirit (who by chance or by error or necessity would have gone astray in matter). He is at once and consubstantially individual and person, dependent on material heredity and spiritual values. Without neglecting its primary task of awakening the mind, the school respectful of human wholeness also recognizes the importance of physical education for a well-balanced human being, pays attention to sense perception, imagination, feeling, to the development "of hands and of the mind", etc.[4]

That is why in addition to the subjects which make up part of the study category (they constitute the very substance of the teaching program), Maritain recognizes the essential, although secondary, role of "play" taken in a broad sense: "it possesses a value and worth of its own, being the activity of free expansion and a gleam of poetry in the very field of those energies which tend by nature toward utility" (C, 55). In this play category, we find games themselves, sports and physical education, manual work and handicrafts (e.g. gardening and home economics), "accomplishments"... These activities should find a place in the primary and secondary schools. "All of these things are dignified if they are dealt with as play activity, not with too much seriousness or too many frowns, but with some free and poetical cheerfulness" (C, 55).

However, Maritain focuses his attention on the primary task of the school, that is, on the intellectual life and the teaching programs.

B. THE STAGES OF SCHOOL EDUCATION

In this respect, Maritain bases his pedagogical proposals — without however referring explicitly to theories in educational psychology concerning mental development — on what he calls the principal stages of education namely: the *rudiments* (or elementary education); the *humanities* (or secondary education); *advanced studies* (or university education). "And these periods correspond not only to three chronological periods in the growth of the youth but also to three naturally distinct and qualitatively determinate spheres of psychological development, and, accordingly, of knowledge" (C, 58).

---

[3] EM, 56-59.
[4] EM, 129-133.

In fact, knowledge does not exist outside of man; the different kinds of knowledge are "vital and internal energies" of the mind and "must develop therefore according to the inner spiritual structure of the mind in which they have their being" (C, 59). The temptation towards *intellectual dwarfing* is strong following the opinion that it would suffice to simplify, the knowledge and sciences of adults and to present them *in miniature form* for the sake of children and the youth. "So we try to cram young people with a chaos of summarized adult notions which have been either condensed, dogmatized, and textbookishly cut up or else made so easy that they are reduced to the vanishing point. As a result, we run the risk of producing either an instructed, bewildered intellectual dwarf, or an ignorant dwarf playing at dolls with our science" (C, 59).

Yet, as to the way of knowing, the thinking of the child is "intrinsically and basically different from that of the adult", each having its own qualities and capable of attaining its perfection.

"The universe of a child is the universe of imagination — of an imagination which evolves little by little into reason." In this regard, the child's mentality resembles that of primitive man and tends toward magic; the child's knowledge exists "in a state of story" and it is "an imaginative grasp of the things and values of the world". The role of the teacher toward this age of the mind will be to "progressively tame the imagination to the rule of reason" and the inspiring power of his pedagogy will be *beauty*. "Beauty makes intelligibility pass unawares through sense-awareness. It is by virtue of the allure of beautiful things and deeds and ideas that the child is to be led and awakened to intellectual and moral life" (C, 61). It is in the mental atmosphere of beauty that the already lively intuitiveness of the child takes its leaps with "a kind of bounding, temperamental, and lucid freedom" only awaiting the exercise of reason in order to be strengthened.

The mental universe of the adolescent is a transitional universe, — a restless and moving universe — between the intuitiveness of the child and the knowledge of the adult, the universe of an intellect "eager to pass judgment on everything, and both trustful and exacting, and which craves intuitive sight" (C, 62). The adolescent thirsts for universal truth, not for the universality appropriate to adult specialization, for it is not yet a question of the development of the mind resulting from the acquisition of intellectual virtues (that is the intellect in so far as it is scientifically formed and equipped), but a *universal knowledge* at the level of the *natural intelligence*.[5] The objective of this universal knowledge is not the acquisition of science itself or art itself, but "the grasp of their *meaning* and the comprehension of the truth or beauty they yield. It is less a question of sharing in the very activity of the scientist or the poet than of nourishing oneself intellectually on the results of their achievement" (C, 63). At the termination of these secondary (pre-

---

[5]   "At this level of natural intelligence, the youth can be offered, not scientific knowledge supposedly reduced and concentrated, but some real, integrated, and articulate, though imperfect understanding — what Plato would have called 'right opinion' — about the nature and meaning of that knowledge which is proper to men in possession of the intellectual virtues" (EM, 49).

university) studies, the youth will not be a scientist, a philosopher, or an artist, but he will have a cultivated mind and will have acquired a truly general culture. "The practical condition for all that is to strive to penetrate as deeply as possible into the great achievements of the human mind rather than to tend toward material erudition and atomized memorization... Thus college education can keep its necessary character of comprehensive universality and at the same time till and cultivate the whole mind, made available and alive, for the tasks of man" (C, 63).

This general culture for everyone should allow each youth — especially those who will immediately take a job or will prepare themselves for professional training — to attain a sufficient intellectual development so that he can "pursue his education and broader his culture his whole life long, according to each one's capacities, thanks to reading, the theatre, concerts, the cinema, etc., and to the good use of leisure time" (PE, 79).

Finally, the third and last level of intellectual development allows the mind to acquire those special energies called intellectual virtues, it is the stage of the intense specialization of a "scientifically" formed mind in which "the intellectual virtues reach their completion" (PE, 128). It is the stage of adult knowledge in which specialized knowledge must be accompanied by a deepening of liberal education and a broadening of general culture requiring professors "themselves to have the sense of the connections and correspondences which exist between all the different regions of the universe of knowledge and to communicate this to the students, put in another way, to make them see, by the flame which animates them, that the intellectual virtues are sister-virtues under the sky of the transcendentals" (PE, 91). According to Maritain, this specialized knowledge is the proper realm of the Universities and professional Schools; in contrast to the general knowledge of secondary education, this specialized knowledge should only be made available to those who are gifted for intellectual work.

So, then, according to Maritain, there are three stages of education corresponding to the three great stages of the development of the intellect.[6]

There is first of all the *awakening of the intellectual powers,* especially the awakening of the intuitiveness of the mind which emerges through the world of imagination; the responsibility for it rests primarily on the elementary school where the rudiments of knowledge are taught.

The second stage is that of the secondary school, the *humanities* where — prior to any specialization — the natural intellect is developed in the direction of universal knowledge by way of "right opinion". This is basic liberal education, *normally for everyone.* This education should allow each

---

[6]   "The general plan which I have in mind and which forms the background of my present considerations divides the main educational periods as follows: I. The rudiments (or elementary education): 7 years, divided into 4 years of initial elementary education (age: six to nine) and 3 years of complementary elementary education (age: ten to twelve). II. The humanities: 7 years, divided into 3 years of secondary education or high school (age: thirteen to fifteen) and 4 years of college education (age: sixteen to nineteen). III. Advanced studies, comprising the university and higher specialized learning (C, 67).

citizen, by reason of his general culture, to acquire an intellectual autonomy sufficient to enable him to continue to instruct himself during his leisure time and enabling him to fulfill his social responsibilities in a clear-headed and critical way.

The third stage is that of the perfecting of the intellect by "specialized knowledge", at the University and professional Schools. This perfecting will be liberating if it is animated by the spirit of universality and accompanied by a deepening of general culture.

Maritain has not dealt with the programs of the elementary school in an explicit way, but he has clearly presented his views concerning the curricula of secondary (pre-university) schools and universities.

II.- THE SECONDARY SCHOOL: LIBERAL EDUCATION FOR ALL

"In a social order fitted to the common dignity of man, college education should be given to all, so as to complete the preparation of the youth before he enters the state of manhood" (C, 64). Secondary education, obtained through "studies which are normal for all" does not have as its objective the formation of future specialists in the different branches of knowledge, anymore than the formation of future professors; it does not speak to the adolescent as a member of a privileged class. Its aim is to form *all future citizens* — therefore all the youth — by making them able "to think in a genuinely free and liberating manner" (EM, 48).

Maritain contends that this is why the introduction of specialization in the secondary school is a serious pedagogical mistake and deprives the youth of a basic right, the right to receive a liberal and universal education preparing them better than any other "for human work and for human leisure" and which is also the privileged foundation of specialization whether it be technical, vocational or university. The humanities do not directly prepare one for the labour market: "no one is predestined to a definite profession" (PE, 130).[7] The humanities have as their goal assisting all human beings to assume their vocation as man and citizen in an autonomous way by rendering them "able to make sound and independent judgments in new and changing situations, either with respect to the body politic or to their own particular task" (EM, 75).[8]

As a result "all the citizens of a country have the right, because they are men, to a pre-university liberal education" (PE, 80).

---

[7]   See also C, 18-20. As the Faure Report establishes, job mobility in addition makes this general training more imperative. *Learning to Be,* p. XXVII-XXVIII.

[8]   "It is also to be expected that these future citizens would educate their children and discuss with them competently the matters taught in school. Moreover, it is assumed that they would dedicate their own leisure time to those activities of rest through which man enjoys the common heritage of knowledge and beauty, to those activities of superabundance through which he helps his fellow-men with generosity" (EM, 75).

A. THE MARITAINIAN CONCEPT OF THE HUMANITIES

How then are we to conceptualize the liberal arts (or humanities) in order that they will effectively foster the progressive conquest of the freedom of autonomy — at least at the level of knowledge and the intellect?

Maritain proposes a serious recasting of the concept of the humanities and liberal arts taking into account human advancement in recent centuries and allowing the young intellect to nourish itself on great human achievements: "I submit that the humanities are those disciplines which make man more human, or nurture in man his nature as specifically human, because they convey to him the spiritual fruit and achievements of the labor of generations, and deal with things which are worth being known for their own sake, for the sake of truth or the sake of beauty" (EM, 84).

Therefore the field of the humanities should be enlarged, in order to include the achievements of the human mind in the sciences as in literature and the arts thereby ceasing to be almost exclusively literary.[9] The list of subjects included in the secondary curriculum will be given in the next section — section B — but Maritain, without wanting in any way to neglect the humanities in the traditional sense, includes "physics and the natural sciences, the history of sciences, anthropology and the other human sciences, with the history of cultures and civilizations, even technology (in so far as the activity of the spirit is involved), and the history of manual work and the arts, both the mechanical and fine arts" (EM, 69).

Essentially the sciences must be taught for the love of knowledge, not, at first, from the viewpoint of the possibility they offer man to become "master and possessor of nature". They "provide man with a vision of the universe and a sense of the sacred, exacting, unbending objectivity of the humblest truth, which play an essential part in the liberation of the mind and in liberal education" (EM, 70). The history of the sciences — their genesis, progress, and vicissitudes — can give to the student a more accurate understanding of scientific truth and its real scope. And then, surely, the human sciences can afford him a better knowledge of human nature and its development.

Obviously, the different components of the liberal arts — literature, history, art, science, etc. — should not be taught in a way to form specialists in each subject but rather for the purpose of general culture; "the objective is less the acquisition of science itself or art itself than the grasp of their meaning and the comprehension of the truth or beauty they yield. It is less a question of sharing the very activity of the scientist or the poet than of nourishing oneself intellectually on the results of their achievement" (C, 63).[10]

---

[9] The general culture that Maritain proposes "does not mention either Latin or Greek: in my opinion, they would represent chiefly a waste of time for the many destined to forget them; Latin, Greek, and Hebrew (or at least one of these three root-languages of our civilization) should be learned later on — much more rapidly and fruitfully — by graduate students in languages, literature, history or philosophy" (C, 69-70).

[10] "Let me stress once again at this point that the objective of basic liberal education is not the acquisition of science itself or art itself, and of the intellectual virtues involved, but rather the grasp of their *meaning* and the comprehension of the truth and beauty they yield, a grasp of which natural intelligence is capable and for which it thirsts" (EM, 97).

Liberal education then has the characteristic of comprehensive universality comparable "to the trend of the first thinkers of ancient Greece toward an undifferentiated world of science, wisdom, and poetry", and completely connatural with "common sense and the spontaneous pervasiveness of natural insight and reasoning" (C, 62)[11] in the adolescent and his mental universe.

B. THE CURRICULUM IN SECONDARY EDUCATION

In order to realize the objectives of humanistic formation — taking into account the broadening of the concept of liberal arts — Maritain proposes a rather precise program of secondary education, spread over seven years of study and including two phases: a first phase of three years designed for adolescents from ages 13 to 15 and called *the first years of the humanities,* and the second phase of the *college years* lasting four years (that is from age 16 to 19).

a) *The First Years of the Humanities*

The first three years of the secondary course are a preparation for the liberal arts properly speaking and include "those matters the knowledge of which concerns the intellectual instruments and logical discipline required for the achievements of reason, as well as the treasure of factual and experiential information which must be gathered in memory" (C, 56). In the realm of the pre-liberal arts, therefore, Maritain puts two subject categories: *firstly,* grammar, logic and the languages which are the instruments of thought; *secondly,* history (national history, history of mankind and civilization, history of science) and collateral subjects like geography, astronomy, botany and zoology. All these subjects will be taught during the first phase of secondary studies, with the exception of logic which will take its place during the first year of the second phase. Maritain has even taken care to divide them in a curriculum which it is useful to reproduce here.[12]

> The year of *Languages,* comprising: first, foreign languages, studied in connection with the national language; second, comparative grammar and the art of expression; third, national history, geography, and natural history (especially elementary astronomy and geology).
>
> The year of *Grammar,* comprising: first, grammar, especially comparative grammar and philology; second, foreign languages and the art of expression; third, national history, geography, natural history (expecially botany).
>
> The year of *History and Expression,* comprising: first, national history, history of civilization, the art of expression; second, foreign languages; third, comparative grammar and philology, geography, natural history (especially zoology).

b) *The College Years*

Now it is a matter of instructing adolescents in the liberal arts properly speaking; these seven arts include "those matters the knowledge of which

---

[11] Probably it is one of the reasons why the Greek humanities have always had such a great importance in traditional secondary education.

[12] C, 66, note 2.

refers directly to the creative or perceptive intuition of the intellect'' (C, 56), regrouped in a *trivium* and a *quadrivium* which are a recasting of the list established by Boethius in the Middle Ages.[13] Maritain's *trivium* includes eloquence, literature and poetry, and the fine arts and concern the creative activity of the mind and beauty. The *quadrivium* relates to the truth to be perceived and therefore to knowing and rational activity; it includes mathematics, physical and natural sciences, philosophy and ethics (with allied subjects).

Now here is how the liberal arts are divided in a four year curriculum whose proper power should be ''to raise a man''; it is the second phase of secondary or pre-university studies.[14]

The year of *Mathematics and Poetry,* comprising: first, mathematics, and literature and poetry; second, logic; third, foreign languages, and the history of civilization.

The year of *Natural Sciences and Fine Arts,* comprising: first, physics and natural science; second, fine arts, mathematics, literature and poetry; third, history of the sciences.

The year of *Philosophy* comprising: first, philosophy, that is to say, metaphysics and philosophy of nature, theory of knowledge, psychology; second, physics and natural science; third, mathematics, literature and poetry, fine arts.

The year of *Ethical and Political Philosophy,* comprising: first, ethics, political and social philosophy; second, physics and natural science; third, mathematics, literature and poetry, fine arts, history of civilization and history of the sciences.

It is fitting to add some considerations on the teaching of philosophy and the important place that Maritain reserves for it in his pre-university curriculum; this teaching takes place during the last two years of the program.[15] For philosophy has an eminently humanistic value and can fill an important role in intellectual formation, in liberal education. ''Philosophy, taken in itself, is above utility and for this very reason philosophy is of the utmost necessity for men. It reminds them of the supreme utility of those things which do not deal with means, but with ends'' (UP, 6).[16]

---

[13]   According to Boethius, the *trivium* comprised grammar, rhetoric and logic, while arithmetic, astronomy, geometry and music formed the *quadrivium* (see C. 71, note 3).

[14]   See C, 67-68. In order to be complete, let us add that the program of the last two years should include optional studies in theology (see C, 68, note 1, and 73-75).

''Nobody can do without theology, at least a concealed and unconscious theology, and the best way of avoiding the inconveniences of an insinuated theology is to deal with theology that is consciously aware of itself'' (C, 74).

''...to understand such a science, it is necessary that the soul be well disposed, and for the sake of theology it is not advisable to impose its study on whoever has shown himself unworthy of it by not voluntarily seeking it'' (PE, 89).

[15]   The teaching of philosophy fills an important place in the secondary and pre-university program: philosophy was one of the most important subjects of the final year of the French baccalaureate; the ''classical course'' in French Canada comprised an important philosophical education spread over two years (that were called philosophy years) and which crowned so to speak the humanities. Under numerous influences, this education has crumbled during the last fifteen years.

[16]   In society, philosophy bears witness to Truth and Freedom.

''The philosopher who in pursuing his theoretical task pays no attention to the interests of men, or of the social group, or of the state, reminds society of the absolute and unbending character of Truth.

''As to Freedom, he reminds society that freedom is the very condition for the exercise of thought.'' *On the Use of Philosophy,* pp. 8-9.

Moreover the importance of philosophy finds a natural echo in the mind of each human person, for "there exists in man a philosophic eros and a nostalgia for philosophy" (PG, 104). For the human mind can only truly be cultivated if it aims towards wisdom, since it begs for wisdom; and is not one of the highest goals of liberal education the quest for and, if possible, the acquisition of the foundations of wisdom, which indeed is the philosopher's role. "Philosophy, let us say more precisely metaphysics, is a wisdom. It has a universal object and ultimately all men, at least all cultivated men, need it" (RI, 337).

Anyway, no one can do without philosophy, and everyone "philosophizes" in one way or another, somewhat like Monsieur Jourdain spoke prose without knowing it. Who does not perceive the fallacy hidden under this objection?[17] Would it be the mark of a cultivated mind to let its natural and deep aspiration for philosophical reflection lie fallow? If it is true that no one can do without philosophy, then we should draw from this the only conclusion which forces itself on us and seriously devote ourselves to the study of philosophy, for "the only way of avoiding the damage wrought by an unconscious belief in a formless and prejudiced philosophy is to develop a philosophy consciously" (C, 72). If general culture is obtained by a vital participation in great human achievements, then how could the neglect of philosophy be allowed which is one of the noblest achievements of the mind. "Without knowing philosophy and the achievements of the great thinkers it is utterly impossible for us to understand anything of the development of mankind, civilization, culture, and science" (C, 72).

Obviously, during the secondary and pre-university course, it is not a matter of forming specialists in philosophy, but of contributing in a clearheaded and appropriate way to the humanistic formation of the future citizen.[18]

Here a difficult question arises. Is it possible to reconcile this mental formation which must be animated by truth — "a good philosophy should be a true philosophy" — with the pluralism which reigns in the philosophical world?[19] "First, there is a common, though unformulated, heritage of philosophical wisdom which passes through any real teaching of philosophy, whatever may be the system of the teacher" (C, 72-73).

---

[17]   Yet it is one of the arguments used by those who want to cut back the number of philosophy courses or to make them merely optional. All professors, they say, do a bit of philosophy within the framework of their courses...

[18]   "Besides his properly scientific and demonstrative work, and so addressed especially to experts, it is fitting that the philosopher present the fruit of his labours to the educated public, to 'evervone', but by employing a method of exposition which can only arise then from the art of persuasion (dialectic in the Aristotelian sense) and which aims at generating true opinion rather than science in the soul. It is for this reason that Plato and Aristotle wrote their dialogues" (RI, 338).

[19]   "...a doctrine essentially grounded in truth *is possible,* can only be understood correctly if we recognize at the same time the pluralism of philosophic doctrines, I don't say as normal *de jure,* but as *bound to happen* or normal *de facto:* by reason of the conditions under which human subjectivity is working among philosophers" (PG, 96).

It should be recalled that, for Maritain, the great philosophers have all contributed, each in his way, to the treasury of the *Philosophia Perennis:* "with every great philosopher and every great thinker there is a central intuition which in itself does not mislead" (RT, 60). On the other hand, "teachers in philosophy are not teaching to be believed but in order to awaken reason; and the students in philosophy owe it to their teacher to free themselves from him" (C, 73).

How are we to achieve an educational objective so important and at the same time so difficult?

Philosophical reflection must nourish itself on the experience of life and science, an experience the young either do not have or have in small measure. Maritain suggests beginning by some historical clarifications on the major problems of philosophy; "such a historical description, pointing less at history than at making clear the inner logic and development of the human awareness of these problems, is a kind of vicarious personal experience" (C, 73). This first course in basic philosophical problems would be completed by "a course in the history of philosophy, intent on bringing out the central intuition in which every great system originates and the more often than not wrong conceptualization which makes these systems irreducibly antagonistic" (EM, 140).[20]

C. The Discourse on Method of Secondary Education

Maritain has enlarged the field of liberal education in order to give it a more universal character which corresponds to the advancement of human culture; the curriculum that he proposes testifies to it. But "the quality of the mode or style is of much greater moment than the quantity of things taught, it constitutes the very soul of teaching and preserves its unity and makes it alive and buoyant" (C, 62-63).

It is necessary that the educator always keep in mind the objective itself of secondary education and the humanities, an objective which is not the specialization of the university, but rather *general culture* with its characteristic "of comprehensive universality" allowing the opening of the mind and to "till and cultivate the whole mind, made available and alive, for the tasks of man" (C, 63).

In this regard, Maritain has furnished precious indications on the way of feeding the adolescent's intellect with the results of different disciplines, to make him grasp the meaning and comprehension of the truth and beauty which they dispense, and to place the mind in a state to think, not to weigh it down, in a word, to free the mind.

"In short, the guiding principle is less factual information and more intellectual enjoyment. The teaching should be concentrated on awakening

---

[20]   Maritain suggests that the first course be taught in Christian colleges "in the perspective of Christian philosophy" *(ibid.).* And he hopes that "Aristotelian and Thomistic philosophy, will gain momentum among their fellow men, at least in the generation to come" (C, 73).

But "truths keeps pace with freedom". In *The Peasant of the Garonne* he expresses his lack of sympathy for Canon 1366 #2, (p. 246) prescribing Thomism in the seminaries.

the minds to a few basic intuitions or intellectual perceptions in each particular discipline, through which what is essentially illuminating as to the truth of things learned is definitely and unshakably possessed" (EM, 72).[21] This fundamental pedagogical principle of secondary teaching is based on the very nature of human knowledge. Intellectual development has its beginning and its end in intuition; there is a judgment at the beginning and at the end of reasoning. This pedagogical principle is also based on faith in the value of the human intellect which is primarily a power of the true and the beautiful; the productions of the great humanists are confirmations of this.

What could be more natural than to direct secondary studies toward a vital participation in the privileged experiences of mankind in its great achievements. In this regard, the preferred pedagogical instrument — but not excluding others — is the *reading of great books*.[22] This is obvious when it concerns literature and poetry; the reading and direct examination of books written by some of the great philosophers is no less essential, and this also applies to a certain extent in the realm of the sciences. Reading a great book is sharing in truth and beauty by allowing oneself to be invaded so to speak by the intellectual genius of a great writer (literary figure, poet, philosopher, scientist, historian etc.). It is opening the mind to the dimensions of an intellectual experience of very great value and nourishing oneself on it. "This nevertheless, it seems to me, is all the more profitable as the books in question are not too many in number and therefore may be seriously and lovingly scrutinized, and as they depend, I mean in part, on the free choice of the student" (C, 70).

The last part of the passage quoted presupposes a certain flexibility in the arrangement of the curriculum. In fact, Maritain acknowledges the value of *some specialization* during the second phase of the secondary and pre-university course.

But before dealing with this question, it might be useful to state the way Maritain looks at the teaching of the first phase of the secondary courses (for adolescents from 13 to 15 years old). "During high school years, the mode of teaching would be adapted to the freshness and spontaneous curiosity of budding reason, stirred and nourished by the life of the imagination" (EM, 72).[23] As a consequence, Maritain suggests that in the course of these years the order of teaching should follow *the order of discovery,* which "is

---

[21] This is the principle that has inspired Maritain in the organization of philosophy courses at the secondary level.

[22] "The liberal arts are the arts of freedom. To be free a man must understand the tradition in which he lives. A great book is one which yields up through the liberal arts a clear and important understanding of our tradition... It must follow that if we want to educate our students for freedom, we must educate them in the liberal arts and in the great books." Robert M. HUTCHINS, *Education for Freedom*, p. 14.

[23] This method seems quite appropriate for teaching the subjects of these three years, let us say for instance history, geography, astronomy, botany, zoology. The usefulness of the Socratic method is even more evident for teaching the subjects of the second phase, for this method can greatly assist the development of the critical mind, especially during the two years of philosophy.

experiential-inductive and rational-intuitive rather than inductive and dialectical'' (C, 72). The effort required for the teacher to meet the mind of the adolescent in its freshness and natural spontaneity — the concern with the interior — in order to make him partake of the fruit of great conquests of the mind is incontestable.

Now, if we return to the problem of specialization in the secondary school, in the first place we should reiterate that Maritain rejects the elective system as such and condemns premature specialization of "the education normal for all" (PE, 78) as contrary to the very spirit of liberal education and general culture. Moreover, hasty specialization is of little use in his opinion for "no one is predestined to a definite profession" (PE, 149) and, moreover, any subsequent specialization will be all the more successful as it will be based on a truly general culture, on a "universal formation".[24]

For all that the possibility of progressive specialization during the second part of secondary and pre-university studies is not excluded, "but this kind of specialization is merely that which the temperament, gifts, and inclinations of the youth himself spontaneously provide" (C, 64). By taking into account the actual possibilities of the adolescent, without however ruling out other areas, the pupil is directed and encouraged in the subject areas where he exhibits talent and zeal. This conforms to the spirit of any genuine education consisting in encouragement, in achieving a human awakening as integral as possible.

This should not be seen as a return to the elective system by a roundabout way.[25] For the specialization suggested by Maritain would not be carried out through the exclusion of certain essential subjects; each student must go through "the entire field of those human possibilities and achievements which compose liberal education" (C, 65). Maritain, without giving up the universality of liberal education, offers a program with its contours adapted to the diversity of developing individual natures. "I mean that all the students would have to attend courses in all the matters of the curriculum in basic liberal education; but on the one hand, the apportionment of the hours given to certain of these courses might be different for the students in the various schools of oriented humanities; and on the other hand, special courses in each of these schools would enlighten the student on the vital relationship between the particular discipline being taught and the chief disciplines of the common curriculum. Thus, the essential hierarchy of values inherent in liberal education would be preserved, with the main emphasis, as to the disciplines, on philosophy; and as to the ways and methods, on the reading of great books" (EM, 73-74).

---

[24]   "As a matter of fact, a young man will choose his speciality for himself and progress all the more rapidly and perfectly in vocational, scientific, or technical training in proportion as his education has been liberal and universal" (C, 64).

[25]   "Of course, the rejection of the elective system does not imply that in addition to the essential (and therefore required) subjects of the curriculum other subjects should not be taught in optional courses, chosen by students according to their own preferences" (C, 65).

The realization of this objective would be inspired by considerations relating to the category of play in contrast to that of study (C, 55-56). Maritain is convinced that the boredom generated in some young people by the study of the humanities does not emanate from their inability to acquire a solid general culture, but rather from the fact that these subjects constitute the object of *formal teaching* to which they are more or less allergic.

That is why the quality of education should not be diluted; according to Maritain, the course should be adapted to the level of the more gifted students, with the freedom to add additional help outside of the course for those who would have any difficulty keeping up with the teaching pace.[26] Anymore than subjects essential for general formation optional should be made optional.

Rather the solution of this problem would be located in an informal and unsystematic pedagogical approach. "I think that the interest in matters even primary in importance may be awakened thanks to the activities of play, whose field consequently should be considerably extended, so that we gave them a place (under a secondary heading) in the *work outside the program* appropriate for the life of the secondary school and the study of the humanities" (PE, 174).[27]

In this context, discussion groups bearing on a great book, on a theatrical performance, a concert, etc... would be of considerable pedagogical value as "a preparation for having the adult worker make profitable use of his leisure time" (EM, 153).

These pedagogical reflections offered by Maritain while excusing himself for "giving way to his dreams" (PE, 175), would deserve — as well as his considerations on the program of the humanities — being seriously studied by those preoccupied with the quality of secondary education. To Maritain's dream we could add that of the establishment "of a Maritain experimental school" inspired by his personalist philosophy of education and freedom and organized after the school program and pedagogical methods he proposes. Was there not a Dewey experimental school?

III.- ADVANCED STUDIES AND THE IDEAL UNIVERSITY

As the development of the mind in the secondary and pre-university school is realized by means of the liberal arts and general culture, it is consequently normal that every human person have access to it and cultivates his mind in such a way that he can possess the means needed to live humanly as regards his work, his leisure activities, and his social and political responsibilities and so to continue to extend his culture and instruct himself

---

[26]   Maritain sees an opportunity there for mutual assistance between students who could regroup themselves in free teams "with a view to studies" (PE, 173).

[27]   "Art and poetry offer many possibilities from this point of view. Many a question of logic could be presented, no longer in a didactic form, but as puzzles to resolve for the amusement of the mind. And one could even imagine cases arising from concrete life the discussion of which by way of play would touch on the problems of moral philosophy or on metaphysical problems, to which it would spontaneously awaken thought" *(ibid.)*.

throughout his whole life. This liberal education for all is the normal response of the school to the thirst for knowledge engraved in the heart of every human being. "This thirst for knowledge, for liberal knowledge, is one with the thirst for social liberation and coming of age" (C, 90).[28]

However, this is not the case with advanced studies which have to deal with *advanced intellectual specialization;* they require particular qualities of those who go in for them and, consequently, they are not intended for everyone indiscriminately. According to Maritain, it is for this reason that the diploma of secondary and pre-university studies does not by itself constitute a claim to advanced studies or "a letter of admission to the university". An entrance examination should be required of candidates for these advanced studies, and a selection made according to rather rigorous criteria. "All the citizens of a country have the right, because they are men, to pre-university liberal education. Because of the particular qualifications that it demands of students as well as teachers, the university is not for everyone, far from it" (PE, 80).[29]

So strict a selection process on the part of a philosopher strongly attached to democratic values might be surprising. Does he not proclaim at every opportunity the principle of universal admissibility to the University? It is important to recall that the democracy which Maritain calls for has nothing to do with *leveling* or *mediocrity;* rather it is essentially an organic democracy which must foster the development and freedom of persons according to their real possibilities.

On the other hand, Maritain suggests arrangements marked by flexibility to facilitate the pursuit of university studies for all those (young men or young women) who are gifted for intellectual work and eager for it: the multiplication of academic scholarships and student loans, university extension and evening courses. He even foresees that part-time studies will have a growing importance "in proportion as economic progress will generally reduce working time and thus enable those who want to do so to use more easily the facilities of evening courses" (C, 83).[30]

Advanced studies are surely *specialized studies;* that is even their proper characteristic. "The intellectual virtues acquired by one student are not those acquired by another, be it a question of techniques, useful arts, and applied sciences, or of practical sciences dealing with human life or of speculative sciences. The knowledge which has to develop during university years is

---

[28]   Those who are acquainted with working youth and labor know that nowhere is a greater thirst for knowledge to be found, if only sufficient facilities are given them" *(ibid.).*

[29]   The application of selection criteria is sometimes difficult, particularly when it concerns adults. Some universities prefer the *probationary* admission of adult students, which delays selection until the termination of a first year of university studies (or the equivalent) so that the student must have been successful in order to be given the status of a regular student.

[30]   Maritain has not explicitly dealt with the role of the university with the ever greater number of adults who, without looking for a university specialization culminating in a diploma, desire to round off their culture by benefitting from university resources, "this universe of adult thought" whose subsidies are provided through public funding. The experience of English and French universities in the field of adult education is quite significant.

knowledge in a state of a perfected and rational grasping of a particular subject matter'' (C, 79). This specialization would risk shrinking the intellectual horizon of the university student and unduly limit the life of the mind by confining it within the limits of a defined field of knowledge unless at the same time *"a deepening of liberal education and a broadening of general culture"* (PE, 79) were combined with this intense specialization.

Thus, at the higher level, the liberation of the mind, is realized in the symbiosis of a highly specialized formation and ''the spirit of generalization''.[31]

In the world of the mind, specialized knowledge fills a role analogous to that of a particular function in a living organism; it only has meaning in relation to the whole. So in the university ''the spirit of teaching is a spirit of universality'' and ''consequently requires professors themselves to have the sense of the connections and correspondences which exist between all the different regions of the universe of knowledge and to communicate this to the students, put in another way, to make them see, by the flame which animates them, that the intellectual virtues are sister-virtues under the sky of the transcendentals'' (PE, 91).

Here as in the other sectors of human life, a good way not to substitute the part for the whole and avoid reductionism is to have a mind open to the whole, while cultivating the part. The achievement of this objective presupposes a university organization and a way of teaching inspired by the spirit of universality.

A. THE IDEAL UNIVERSITY

In *Education at the Crossroads,* Maritain sets forth the architecture of the ideal university based on an integral and integrated vision of specialized studies. "It is suitable that actually all the arts and sciences, even those which concern the management of common life and the application of the human mind to matters of practical utility, should be embraced by the typical modern university" (C, 76).

This ideal university would be genuinely universal: universal because it would be the place for teaching all specialized knowledge, and because its organization would be conceived "according to the qualitative and internal hierarchy of human knowledge, and because from top to bottom, the arts and sciences would have been grouped and organized according to their growing value in spiritual universality" (C, 77); universal, finally, through the economy of its "interdisciplinary studies".

In the ideal university, the departments or faculties would be replaced by institutes regrouped in four teaching cities. Here is a brief description of them:[32]

---

[31] Maritain is inspired here by Alfred North Whitehead's phrase from the book *The Aims of Education* which is full of suggestions in this regard.

[32] See C, 77-78. The U.E.R. (Unité d'enseignement et de recherche/Teaching and Research Unit) of French universities seems to fill a place analogous to that of the Institutes referred to by Maritain; their regrouping in universities has some similarity with the teaching cities.

Thus a first order of subjects would be concerned with the realm of useful arts and applied sciences in the broadest sense of these words, and with advanced studies in technical training, engineering, administrative sciences, arts and crafts, agriculture, mining, applied chemistry, statistics, commerce, finance, and so on.

A second order would be the realm of those practical sciences — practical either because they belong to the domain of art or because they belong to the domain of ethics — which, though covering thoroughly specialized fields, nevertheless relate to man himself and human life, medicine and psychiatry, for instance, and, on the other hand, law, economics and politics, education, etc.

A third order would be the realm of the theoretical sciences and fine arts, in other words it would be concerned with the liberal arts proper and with that disinterested knowledge of nature and man and of the achievements of culture which liberates the mind by truth or beauty. At this point we find the immense chorus of the free workings of the spirit, mathematics, physics, chemistry, astronomy, geology, biology, anthropology, psychology, pre-history, archeology, history, ancient and modern literature and languages, philology, music, fines arts, and so on. That is the very core of the life of the university and the very treasure of the civilized heritage. And this third order is to culminate in a fourth one, which is the highest animating center in the architecture of teaching, and which deals with those sciences that are also wisdom because they are universal by virtue of their very object and of their very essence: the philosophy of nature, metaphysics and the theory of knowledge, ethical philosophy, social and political philosophy, the philosophy of culture and of history, theology and the history of religions.

But in order that the university live on the comprehensive universality required by the intellectual development of the student (who is a living subject), a co-existence of specialized subject matters is insufficient; multidisciplinary parallelism must be overcome and the way of interdisciplinary studies must be followed. Maritain makes two important recommendations to this end, one relating to the curriculum, the other relating to the intellectual work of the professors.

Whatever his field of specialization may be, the curriculum of each student, should include certain courses in the subjects of the third and fourth teaching orders as obligatory: "Part of these courses, for instance in science, history, ancient and modern literatures, or fine arts, would be a matter of free choice, according to the personal inclination of the student, and to the need for complement or contrast in his special training. Other courses should be required for all, namely general philosophy, ethical and political philosophy, the history of civilization" (C, 80-81).

As to the professors, they should be regrouped in special interdisciplinary committees (that is, made up of professors from different Institutes); these committees would have different functions, especially to ensure ongoing collaboration between their members and to guide the student along the path of interdisciplinary studies. Maritain illustrates this last recommendation by different examples which show how "the spirit of generalization" might be fostered: "for instance, the connections of physics, biology, psychology, or medicine with the history of the sciences, the history of civilization, the philosophy of nature, and the theory of knowledge, or the connections of economics, social sciences, law, education, or of literature and art, with the history of civilization, ethical and political philosophy, and the great metaphysical and theological problems" (C, 81). The encounter with different disciplines would foster as well a vital deepening of specialized knowledge.

B. AN ALTERNATIVE

While proposing the architecture of the ideal university, Maritain had taken care to add a warning concerning the subject matter of the first and second teaching order; the condition of their inclusion in the university is their participation in the spirit of universality. "Everything would be warped if the aim, incentive, and dominating concern of the teaching were directed toward success in the experiences of life and in money-making" (C, 77).[33]

Now, in the new edition of the book *Pour une philosophie de l'éducation* (1969), Maritain expresses some reservations in connection with the ideal university which he considers henceforth as utopian "because it misconstrues and endangers the character of universality which is essential to the university, just as essential as the specialization proper to the acquisition of such and such an intellectual virtue" (PE, 91).

In order that this ideal of university teaching be realized, it is necessary that an education completely impregnated with comprehensive universality reigns in the different specializations found there, an education which tends in a completely disinterested way toward the pure knowledge of the truth. Now, Maritain realizes that the sciences and the arts turned toward the practical life, that is the subject matter of the first two teaching orders of the ideal University, are not adapted to this end.

As a result, Maritain recommends a new organization of advanced studies, since the *ideal University* was based on "an unacceptable confusion between *advanced studies* whatever they may be and the *university*" (PE, 92). The universities will retain the subjects better adapted to the spirit of universality and to disinterested knowledge, that is those of the teaching order of pure knowledge and theoretical, and intrinsically universal knowledge.

And then, alongside of the universities, there will be advanced professional schools and technical schools dedicated to advanced studies in the subjects arising from the first two orders of knowledge: the useful arts, applied sciences and practical sciences, because they have nothing to do with universal knowledge; in these advanced schools "specialization alone reigns supreme" (PE, 80).

But after having grouped higher education into two distinct categories institutions, Maritain insists that a close collaboration exist between these institutions, by virtue indeed of the principle of inter-disciplinary studies and universality, since "the use of technical means cannot be really profitable, nor the practical sciences be well directed without general enlightenment about nature and man" (C, 80). For instance, the professors and students of the Universities and Advanced Schools should meet each other in regular seminars for their mutual benefit. The most general knowledge would clarify

---

[33] "The students may take such motives into consideration when they choose to enter a given course of study. But the curriculum itself must be directed only toward a sound and comprehensive organization of universal knowledge, to be taught according to the internal and objective structure of the parts thereof" *(ibid.)*.

the specialized knowledge of a practical order and the data of experience from the practical disciplines would stimulate the reflections of university people by binding them more closely to what is concrete.

According to Maritain, this alternative necessitated by a more rigorous application of the principle of universality in the University doesn't alter his basic philosophy of higher education which requires that specialized teaching be complemented by the *spirit of universality,* so important if the trap of reductionism is to be avoided, and to free the mind and direct it toward wisdom. What is important, above and beyond administrative structures — without in any way ignoring their influence in this context — is the decompartmentalization of advanced curricula and their re-orientation toward inter-disciplinary studies, which by all indications requires the decompart-mentalization of minds (particularly in the professoriat).

C. COMPLEMENTS OF UNIVERSITY EDUCATION

Advancement in specialized knowledge, particularly in the scientific realm, presupposes original research which cannot be carried out without creating a state of tension in the professors, between the demands of university teaching and necessary research whose importance for the progress of science and civilization is obvious.

"In the nature of things, the object of universities is the teaching of youth, and not producing books and articles and endless contributions, or making some scientific, philosophical, or artistic discovery" (C, 84). This does not exclude any research from teaching, far from it; but the university professor who dedicates himself seriously and deeply to specialized knowledge which is the object of his teaching as well as to the vital links with other kinds of knowledge, and who is concerned about the education of his students "by means of courses, directed readings, the correction of dissertations, conducting discussion groups or *seminars,* or laboratory training", has little time available for the concentration and continued effort required by "original" inquiry with a view to the advancement of knowledge.

Does it not all too often occur that university teaching is neglected because of exaggerated fostering of university research "detached" from the purposes of teaching.[34]

Maritain sees in "the pretention to replace teaching by research" one of the "stupidities" which were at the origin of the Events of May — June, 1968 in the French university environment.[35]

Many solutions can be considered to reduce the tension between teaching and research. In order to resolve this crucial problem for university life as for the advancement of science, Maritain suggests that university life receive a

---

[34]   "It is no doubt normal that any instruction given in the university will result in some original work and the advancement of knowledge, especially in science. Yet this is in a way an overflow of the teaching scholarship" (C, 84).

[35]   See PE, 119. American and Canadian universities have also had their period of student protest during the years 1968-1969. It is by no means certain that changes in the university resulting from it have gotten to the root of the problem...

necessary complement in the form of research institutes especially devoted to the progress and advancement of science.[36]

Maritain suggests the creation of "schools of spiritual life" as a second complement of university life. As he correctly notes, this kind of regrouping revives an old tradition[37] and calls to mind the Pythagorean and Platonic schools, just to point out two examples from among our intellectual ancestors.

If it is the case that we are living through a crisis of civilization marked by "the complete absence, among free peoples, of a philosophy of life and of the society which would be proper to it" (PE, 113), it is more understandable why Maritain strongly suggests the establishment of these schools of spiritual life or wisdom.

For people of the Christian faith, the creation of centres of spiritual renewal is especially needed, it concerns "houses of hospitality and enlightenment for human souls "where those in charge could stay permanently and those who wished to renew themselves there would be able to come at regular intervals. For instance, they might "lead a common life during some weeks, ... be trained in the ways of spiritual life and contemplation, and ... learn that science of evangelical perfection which is the highest part of theology".[38] The Bible, theology, the great spiritual teachers would be the nourishment dispensed in these centres completely geared towards wisdom and inspired by the appeal of the heroes and the saints, those great educators of mankind.

IV.- THE SCHOOL AND MORAL EDUCATION

The preceding chapter has recalled the role of the school in the realm of moral education.[39] Nevertheless it is important to return to this primordial question. In fact, for the liberation of the person, and the conquest of personal freedom, it is worth more to be good and upright than it is to be learned. Even

---

[36]   In Canadian universities, research constitutes a part of the normal tasks of a professor and there is a tendency, in some circles, to give more importance to research than to teaching.

The Report of a Commission to study the rationalization of university research, published in 1972, states in regard to this issue: "We recommend that the universities revise their policies on promotion and salary increases to ensure that the same weight is given to undergraduate teaching and reflective inquiry as is given to frontier research and teaching and supervision of graduate students." L.-P. BONNEAU and J.A. CORRY, *Quest for the Optimum, Research Policy in the Universities of Canada* (Ottawa: Association of Universities and Colleges of Canada, Vol. I, 1972), pp. 55-56.

[37]   "In China and India, wise men living in solitude and contemplation gather together disciples who come to listen to them either for a certain number of years or at certain seasons of the year. The Hindu *ashrams* or schools of wisdom are well known" (C, 84).

[38]   The Thomist Study Circles organized by the Maritains from 1919 to 1939 in some ways filled the role of a "school in spiritual life". It is both interesting and symptomatic to note the emergence, during the last decade, of groups of university students interested in religious spirituality oriental as well as western and, on another level, the creation of several "Institutes of Values" in American universities. May not some signs of hope in the regeneration of our civilization be discerned in that?

[39]   See above, p. 80.

if we must pay attention both to intellectual development and the development of the will, moral formation is more important than intellectual formation.[40]

Now, the family has a more important direct influence on the moral life of the child than the school does. Yet, the school cannot be indifferent to moral education; in fact the school has to deal with human persons, not pure intellects. How then might the school contribute in a positive way to the moral education of the youth?

A. School Life

Maritain considers the school and the university as a sphere of life in which an apprenticeship must be served in freedom and in moral and social responsibilities. This is why "in a manner adapted to the age and capacity of students, schools and universities should be laboratories in the responsibilities of freedom and the qualities of the mind proper to democratic citizenship" (EM, 68). Common life, school discipline, regulations, school work, etc., are excellent means of moral formation.

In this respect, Maritain suggests the free organization of student teams responsible for the discipline of their members and their progress in school work. These teams would be both teams of mutual assistance in the school work of students and teams having a participatory role in the management of the school; through their representations to school authorities, they would bring suggestions, experiences and problems of the group relating to the organization of studies, general discipline and the political life of the school or university. At the same time, it is the apprenticeship in and the exercise of the moral and social life. It is surely a practical way of understanding and experiencing the needs of democratic life.

B. The Teaching of Morality

But since the school has the life of the intellect as its principal responsibility, its role in regard to the moral life of youth is first and foremost an indirect one and is carried out in the form appropriate to it, that is, through *the teaching of morality*. That is why "the teaching of morality, with regard to its intellectual bases, should occupy a great place in school and college education" (C, 23).

According to Maritain, the normal setting of the teaching of morality is that of religious formation, religious education;[41] now this education at the

---

[40]   "Formation in moral life and virtues is an essential part, indeed the most important part, of the primary aim of education in the broad sense of the word" (EM, 75).

[41]   This is a corollary of the Maritainian position relating to *moral philosophy adequately considered* whose value proceeds from its subordination to the concrete end of man which, in fact, is supernatural according to Christian faith: "whereas in the field of personal morality, the whole scope of the moral life cannot be comprehended by reason with regard to our real system of conduct in actual existence, without taking into account the supratemporal destiny of man" (C, 95).

On this question of moral philosophy adequately considered, see *Science and Wisdom,* pp. 174-220 and pp. 231-241, as well as *An Introduction to Philosophy,* pp. 266-267.

public secondary school would be limited to an optional course in theology given during the first two years of the program. Would that be the only moral education offered in the setting of the secondary school?

Natural morality should have an important place in the humanities program. "Natural morality and the great ethical ideas conveyed by civilization should be taught during these years. They are the very treasure of classical humanism, they must be communicated to the young" (C, 68).

The secondary school has at its disposal two ways of communicating the great moral ideas with which all civilization is impregnated; that is, the teaching of moral philosophy (ethics, political and social philosophy) such as is indicated in the program of the last year of humanities, but also and above all a teaching embodied in the humanities and liberal arts, "especially as an integral part of the teaching of literature, poetry, fine arts, and history" (C, 68).

The entire teaching of the great classical authors is pervaded with moral values; more than any special course in morality, reading authors like Homer, Herodotus, Virgil, Cicero, Saint Augustine, Montaigne, Pascal, etc. "feeds the mind with the sense and knowledge of natural virtues, of honor and pity, of the dignity of man and of the spirit, the greatness of human destiny, the entanglements of good and evil, the *caritas humani generis*" (C, 68-69)[42] The youth can thus instruct themselves and benefit from the moral experience of mankind.

Now, in regard to special courses in moral philosophy, Maritain suggests that, without in any way underrating personal morality, the emphasis should be placed on "the ethics of political life and civilization"; since it is in the domain of temporal activities that natural reason is more at ease, the proper ends of the political order being of a natural order and the virtues relevant to this order being natural virtues.

At this point, Maritain recognizes that the school has a completely determinant role in regards to the foundations of democratic life, that is, "the teaching of the democratic charter". In fact, how is it possible to live in a society of free men if there is no agreement on the very basis of common life? "There are, thus, a certain number of tenets — about the dignity of the human person, human rights, human equality, freedom, justice and law — about which democracy presupposes common consent and which constitute what may be called the democratic charter. Without a general, firm, and reasoned-out conviction concerning such tenets, democracy cannot survive" (EM, 62).

An assent of a *practical order* to this democratic charter is required of everyone in a society which respects the human person in all men and wants to make possible the freedom and the liberation of all. And education has the

---

[42]   The great authors in moral philosophy have also an important contribution to offer in this regard. The important book that Maritain has dedicated to them under the title, *Moral Philosophy, An Historical and Critical Survey of the Great Systems* (New York: Charles Scribner's Sons, 1964), 468 p.

duty not only to foster a knowledge of this democratic credo through teaching, but to foster as well an enlightened and deep conviction in this respect, without which adherence to the democratic character would be baseless and of little value.[43]

Now the theoretical justifications of the democratic charter, that is the world views, conceptions of life, philosophical credos are diversified, and the school cannot impose its viewpoint in this respect, since that would be in fundamental contradiction with the democratic charter itself. "The conclusion is obvious. For the very sake of providing unity in adherence to the democratic charter, a sound pluralism must obtain in the means" (EM, 65). In that way the difficult problem of pluralism in the school is stated and it is while studying the question of the teaching of the democratic charter that Maritain discusses pluralism.

C. PLURALISM IN THE SCHOOL

How to arrange the educational system in such a way that it fills its role in the best way possible respecting the convictions and freedoms of teachers and students, without stooping to indoctrination, but also without being satisfied with a stunted and superficial education?

In the first place, the value of teachers is of paramount importance. It is of supreme importance that those who have teaching duties in regard to moral and social values possess two great complementary qualities: *deep personal convictions* and *an open and generous mind*.[44]

Would it be possible to ensure the emergence of enlightened convictions in the student if the person who teaches doesn't have them? It goes without saying that it is not a matter of fanaticism nor of blind faith in a philosophy of life, but of the intellectual convictions (which result from a serious inquiry) of a well-informed and critical mind which however knows to some extent why it has faith in man, truth, freedom, democracy etc., which may imply *a philosophy* and *a religious faith*.

This first quality must be accompanied by what could be called "the charity of the mind", that is, enough openness of mind and generosity to accept the fact that other professors (and students) have different convictions. Thus the teacher bears living witness to a real "democratic" spirit, that is, respect for persons and their freedom.

Secondly, Maritain wonders what transformation of the school system would allow us to resolve the concrete problem of pluralism in a practical way. In this regard, he offers three possible solutions "at least worthy of being tentatively tried and tested" (EM, 67) for examination.

Apparently Maritain thinks it is relatively easy to resolve the first case, that of schools situated in a homogeneous environment regarding its spiritual traditions. Then teaching of courses in morality should be entrusted to teachers whose personal religious or philosophical convictions would roughly correspond to those of the social environment.

---

[43]   See *Man and the State*, pages 119-126, and *On the Philosophy of History*, pp. 116-117.
[44]   EM, 65-66. Don't we have here two qualities that should be found in any teacher?

If the communities are heterogeneous, an analogous heterogeneity should be found in the teaching personnel of the school so that the pupils could be divided into homogeneous groups, according to the great traditions of that environment.

Finally, if that is not possible, the democratic charter could be taught in a new and purely historical discipline. "The new discipline in question would bring together, in the basic framework of national history and history of civilization, matters pertaining to the humanities, human sciences, social philosophy, and philosophy of law, all these to be centered on the development and significance of the great ideas comprised in the common charter" (EM, 66-67).

It is Maritain's firm conviction that the application of the proposed solutions or "of some pluralistic arrangement" would allow the school system to carry out its educational function in a better way. He even believes that if the public school system were to be inspired with a pluralistic pedagogy of the kind he proposes, it would respond in a better way to the aspirations of Catholic families.[45]

In place of a neutral educational system, there would then be a multiconfessional system, the religious education adapted to the different confessions represented in the school would be possible either through regular courses listed in the time table, or by additional optional courses in an appropriate free period.

V.- CHRISTIAN EDUCATION

Maritain, the Christian philosopher, could not expound his philosophy of education without including in it some considerations on Christian education as such.

Education in the broadest sense is the process of personal development; it is "an integral education for an integral humanism". Now following the Christian conception, the human person is both a natural and a supernatural being and "Christian education does not only lay stress on the natural spirituality of which man is capable, it does not only found its entire work on the inner vitality of human nature; it makes its entire work rest also on the vital energies of grace and on the three theological virtues, Faith, Hope, and Charity; and if it is true to its highest aim, it turns man toward grace-given spirituality, toward a participation in the freedom, wisdom, and love of the saints" (EM, 131).[46]

That is why Christian education must foster the development of the natural virtues (intellectual and moral) and the supernatural virtues, in the respect for personal wholeness.[47] And this education extends over a lifetime

---

[45] PE, 188. It is in this spirit that the seventh chapter of *Pour une philosophie de l'éducation* is written, entitled "L'école publique en France et le principe pluraliste", pp. 177-194.

[46] The schools of spiritual life which were previously mentioned (p. 102) are preoccupied with this highest goal.

[47] Following the beautiful phrase of Saint Thomas Aquinas "grace does not destroy nature; it presupposes and perfects it."

— moreover as any education — and is achieved in a way adapted to each age of life. It "already applies to the child in a way adapted to his condition, and must guide school education as to the general orientation of the educational process and the first beginnings of which the child is capable" (EM, 133). The first requirement of Christian education is to respond to the aspirations of the person, as any authentic education must do, that is help the child to attain his perfection as a man, to conquer his personal and social freedom. Being a Christian is not to devaluate the gifts of nature and the riches of personal and communal life; it is rather to recognize in them their own value, and even to recognize in them a greater value because of their incorporation in supernatural life. From this point of view, it may be said that Maritain has stated before hand the principles of "the Declarations on Christian Education" proclaimed by the Second Vatican Council; the Declaration stresses the dignity of the human person, the right of everyone to an education in response to their personal vocation and assisting them "in the harmonious development of their physical, moral, and intellectual endowments. Surmounting hardships with a gallant and steady heart, they should be helped to acquire gradually a more mature sense of responsibility toward ennobling their own lives through constant effort, and toward pursuing authentic freedom."[48] That is why Christian education aims first of all "at helping a child of man attain his full formation or his completeness as a man" (EM, 133).

Added to this basic and general requirement are the more specific requirements of Christian education which will allow fostering a truly internalized life of faith, hope, and charity, that is, on ever greater personal life of faith, freely chosen and sincerely and lucidly received. Maritain's reflections on this question of Christian education in its own specific quality bear on three complementary aspects: that is *the curriculum in general,* the development of the *Christian intelligence* and the *means of strengthening religious knowledge and the spiritual life.* Maritain examines these questions particularly with reference to secondary and pre-university education and in the setting of the *Christian College.*

A. THE CURRICULUM OF A CHRISTIAN COLLEGE

"Our watchword should be enlargement, Christian-inspired enlargement, not narrowing, even Christian-centered narrowing, of the humanities" (EM, 136). This enlargement consists first of all in preserving and even enlarging the general culture of the courses in the humanities. Christianity addresses itself to everyone — it is not a sect — and Christians should be open to everyone and to everything (except sin). It is essentially universal.

Consequently, the general culture of the Christian college must certainly include the great classical authors, those of the Greco-Roman humanities but also the Christian classics. "The writings of the Fathers of the Church are an integral part of the humanities as well as, or more than, those of the

---

[48]   In *The Documents of Vatican II* (New York: The America Press, 1966), p. 639.

Elizabethan dramatists; St. Augustine and Pascal matter to us no less than Lucretius or Marcus Aurelius'' (EM, 135). The humanities curriculum then must deal with *the whole of human culture*.

Moreover, the perspective and the inspiration of the Christian college must be genuinely universal; the Christian college must be concerned with the achievements of the human mind in every great era of civilization and understand them ''in an authentic philosophical and theological light'' (EM, 136). Philosophy and theology play a sapiential role in regard to the whole of human experience and values.

It will be objected that there is no Christian mathematics, nor Christian sciences, etc., and Maritain agrees with this. What counts in secondary teaching is the spirit of universality which impregnates the whole of education. Now, according to Maritain, the Christian educator who fills his teaching with a genuine Christian spirit does not shrink this universal perspective, but enlarges it to the dimensions of the universal Intelligence and will awake in the student the sense of the Universal. For instance, while teaching mathematics as rigorously as any other teacher, the Christian educator will awake in the student something beyond mathematics: ''first, a sense of the proper place of these disciplines in the universe of knowledge and human thought; second, an unspoken intimation of the immortal value of truth, and of those rational laws and harmony which are at play in things and whose primary roots are in the divine intellect'' (EM, 136-137).

B. THE DEVELOPMENT OF CHRISTIAN INTELLIGENCE

Maritain has faith in the human intellect, faith in its possibilities of progressive assimilation of the truth, faith in its worth. This faith is reinforced by Christian revelation and its teachers. Father Clerissac, Maritain's first spiritual director, liked to say: ''Intelligence is the very basis of Christian life.'' Having already defined the proper role of the school in relation to the development of the intellect, Maritain can therefore only reiterate for the Christian school what he admits for any school. ''It is a sacred obligation for a Christian school or college to keep alive the sense of truth in the student; to respect his intellectual and spiritual aspirations...'' (EM, 137).

Now, in the life of the intellect, there is a crucial realm of values which transcends the empiriological character of the sciences, and should occupy a choice place in a Christian college. Philosophy and theology, ''both of which should be the keystone of the edifice of learning in a Christian college, dedicated as it is, by definition, to wisdom'' (EM, 139).[49] Very special

---

[49]   ''Yet a more general and surprising fact remains, namely the fact of the religious ignorance in our contemporary world of a great number, I would say of a majority of people educated in religious schools and denominational colleges'' (EM, 141-142).

It is far from certain that Catholic colleges have all understood the importance of religious (or theological) education. On the pretext of the primary importance of a Christian atmosphere in the school, a certain number of them have seriously neglected religious teaching. Perhaps they have forgotten the word of Saint Paul: *Fides ex auditu*. Ignorance of the Christian faith is certainly not a solid basis for Christian education and a genuinely Christian life.

attention should be accorded to the teaching of theology which is according to a medieval saying, *fides quaerens intellectum* — a theology capable of nourishing the faith of the Christian and enlightening him about his personal and social responsibilities. To achieve this, theology should combine the deepening of the *revealed datum* with an openness to contemporary problems, problems raised by science, inherent in the social movements of our age, without neglecting the study of comparative religion.

And to better strengthen religious culture in a great spirit of autonomy and openness, Maritain suggests that these courses be completed by "special seminars in which students in philosophy and theology would meet representatives of the most various schools of thought: scientists, artists, missionaries, labor leaders, managers, etc." (EM, 140).

Moreover, the development of "the intelligence of faith" should include a serious study of exegesis as an elective subject for students eager for "Christian intelligence" and wanting with a greater faith to go in "for that assiduous reading of the scriptures which has been a sacred custom in Protestant countries and is now being practiced more and more among Catholics, and which is an invaluable asset of Christian life" (EM, 141).

C. The Means of Strengthening Spiritual Life

The integration of Christian thought in the life of the mind is of very great importance in a Christian college.

The Christian college must also foster "the integration of religious training in the personal life of the students". In this regard, Maritain stresses the absolutely free character of the participation in the proposed activities.

As a sign of the penetration of Christian faith in daily life, it is important that a vibrant liturgy be organized in Christian colleges and on the campuses of Christian universities. This liturgical life could be monitored by liturgical teams. There could also be spiritual life teams directed towards the study of the great theologians and mystics, daily reading of the Gospel, and prayer.

Maritain the contemplative doesn't see any limits to the development of the intellect; it is along the road of the mystical life that Christian education must lead students, at least those who would really want to respond to this appeal. Contemplation is a natural aspiration of the intellect and guides it toward wisdom; Christian wisdom doesn't constitute an exception to that.

Chapter VI

The Relevance of Maritain

In the preceding pages, we have presented to the reader the results of our research into Jacques Maritain's philosophy of education which is an *education for freedom.*

We have read, scrutinized and analyzed with a great deal of sympathy — and with considerable intellectual enjoyment as well — most of Maritain's works in order to discover the basic intuitions in them and to retrace from the inside so to speak his philosophical itinerary beginning with his conception of the person and freedom and continuing to the hard problem of moral education and the Christian school. We have gone through the major questions of the philosophy of education: its aims, the role of the educator, the dynamics of education (the dialectic of the teacher and pupil), the specific role of the school, the spirit and the curriculum of secondary and pre-university education and those of university education.

In his works — especially in his pedagogical writings — Maritain frequently employs the word *freedom,* this word at once so formidable (how many slaves have been made in its name!) and so laden with passion, but whose reality is at the very core of the human person. We believe we have been faithful both to the letter and the spirit of Maritain's pedagogy when styling it *an education for freedom.*

I.- AN EDUCATION FOR FREEDOM

Freedom is the attribute allowing a person to become what he is. "The free act is not only the act of the person as such, it is moreover, — and this is perhaps the same thing, — the revelation of the person to itself" (SP, 137).[1] The freedom at issue is not just the freedom of choice — required at the start — but also and above all the freedom of spontaneity progressively conquered which is autonomy and expansion.

---

[1] "Even taking for granted evolution in the realm of nature, Bergson admits that there is a gulf between animals and man. It is freedom which creates this gulf" (March 1, 1910) (CN, 88).

According to the *Carnet de notes* (p. 187), The Circles of Thomistic Studies which met from 1919 to 1939 were constantly preoccupied studying the problem of freedom: "Free will, the order of exercise and that of specification; the composite and the divided sense; the dominating indifference of the will; the last practical judgment; the analysis of the voluntary act..."

"The most fundamental aspiration of the person is the aspiration towards the liberty of expansion and autonomy" (RM, 27), and *his education* is the process through which each person expresses his effort to conquer this freedom in the personal as in the social order: primarily in the personal order, that of *internal freedom*, for man is more a whole than a part; secondarily (but essentially as well) in the order of social freedom and responsibilities. "Thus the prime goal of education is the conquest of internal and spiritual freedom, or, in other words, his liberation through knowledge and wisdom, good will, and love (C, 11); and the second goal "guiding the development of the human person in the social sphere, awakening and strengthening both his sense of freedom and his sense of obligation and responsibility" (C, 14-15).

Moreover, these two essential goals must always be considered in relation to the wholeness of the person, by reason of his fundamental unity.

If the child needs educators, it is because of the innate indeterminacy of its initial freedom; therefore the authority of the educator corresponds to the right to education which "is nothing else than the duty of the adult to the freedom of the youth" (C, 33).

The paths of freedom are those of *truth* and *love:* the paths of truth — whose end is wisdom — that the mind sees very imperfectly through intuition, but whose multiple ramifications and depth are such that the curve which progressively approaches it (like an asymptote) requires varied efforts at assimilation, at "the mastery of reason over the things learned" and at unity, in the joy of knowing; the path of love which must actually realize personal growth toward the Good in such a way that "in the intimacy of man's activities the weight of the egoistic tendencies diminishes, and the weight of the aspirations proper to personality and its spiritual generosity increases" (C, 35).

The role of the different agents of education is to aid the child, the adolescent, the youth, to educate and awaken himself to what is human, to realize his own progressive liberation in its personal and social dimensions. The family is the educational sphere primarily responsible for the budding of the moral and social life of the child: "it is in the nature of things that the vitality and virtues of love develop first in the family" (C, 96).

On the other hand, "school and college education has indeed its own world, which essentially consists of the dignity and achievements of knowledge and the intellect, that is, of the human being's root faculty. And of this world itself, that knowledge which is wisdom is the ultimate goal" (C, 28), and it is also freedom of exultation.

In order to make somewhat more concrete the role of the school from a philosophical point of view, and taking into account the proper character of each of the three stages of education, Maritain inquires into "what would be the main features of a normal college curriculum, for a Western youth of our day" (C, 66) and how the ideal university should be arranged, the one which would be able to join the necessary specialization of advanced studies with "a deepening of liberal education and a broadening of general culture" (PE, 79). In order to complete the picture, Maritain makes explicit the role of the school in connection with moral education and briefly presents his views on the Christian school.

How is Maritain's philosophy of education to be characterized? Maritain's pedagogy seems to us to be an accurate reflection of his conception of philosophy.

Maritain is as much a Thomist and Christian philosopher in his philosophy of the person and freedom as he is in his philosophy of education which is the extension of it. Could we not rightly say that Maritain's writings on education are a commentary on Saint Thomas Aquinas' *De Magistro* for our time?

But, at the same time, and because of that, his pedagogical thought is open to other philosophies, some of whose conclusions he criticizes without reticence as without fear, but whose basic intuitions he appropriates in a vital way. In this respect, while remaining faithful to his philosophical principles — it could even be said in order to remain faithful to them — he has known how to incorporate certain intuitions of Rousseau, Dewey and Bergson in his thought, just to mention only these three, in order to enrich it. This is possible and even necessary because he is a *philosopher of being* and believes that the intellect is made for truth that being (analogical being) manifests to him; he believes in the possibilities of the human intellect, of all the intellects including the intellects of those whose conclusions he does not share, for "with every great philosopher and every great thinker there is a central intuition which in itself does not mislead" (RT, 60).

In a suggestive comparison between the life of the intellect and the moral life, Maritain attributes to the philosophical intellect four great virtues: rational soundness, exactitude of speech, boldness of gaze and clearness of thought.[2] It seems to us that Maritain possesses these qualities of mind to a high degree of perfection.

The rational soundness of this thought is shown in its remarkable coherence; an extended acquaintance with the works of Maritain convinces us of the basic unity and continuity of his philosophy and pedagogical thought.[3] If he enriches his thought with the treasure of great intuitions found in other

---

[2] "It seems to me that corresponding to the virtue of *prudence* (which is in the reason) is this quality of the human intellect which I will call *rational soundness* (then the philosopher is a great organizer of concepts; corresponding to the virtue of *justice* (which is in the will) is the quality of the intellect which I will call *exactitude of speech* (then the philosopher only *states* what he *sees*); corresponding to the virtue of *fortitude* (which is in the irascible appetite) is the quality of the intellect which I will call *boldness of gaze* (then the philosopher is a great intuitive and a great discoverer); corresponding to the virtue of *temperance* (which is in the concupiscible appetite), is the quality of the intellect which I will call *clearness of thought* (then the philosopher is free from the unconscious pressures and cupidities of subjectivity). J. Maritain, "Réflexions sur la nature blessée et sur l'intuition de l'être," in *Revue Thomiste*, Vol. LXVIII, 1968, p. 12).

[3] In answer to criticisms of Maritain which raised doubts about the unity of his thought especially in the philosophy of history, B.W. Smith has written a book in which she successfully shows, in our opinion, the continuity of Maritain's thought, even in this complicated realm of philosophical reflection. The book in question is entitled *Jacques Maritain, Antimodern or Ultramodern, An Historical Analysis of His Critics, His Thought and His Life* (New York, Elsevier, 1976).

philosophers, it is not by a kind of superficial syncretism, but indeed because of the boldness of gaze which originates in the *intuition of being* and broadens to the dimensions of metaphysical realism. Reading Maritain also leads us to discover the clearness of thought which is expressed in phrases sometimes severe and complex, often animated by a great mystical current but where exactitude of speech always breaks through. Maritain states well what he wants to say and clearly expresses himself even if in so doing he allows himself to insert expressions which are sometimes striking and sometimes savory (e.g. the freedom of exultation, the spiritual preconscious, education by the rod, etc.) whose context has quickly allowed us to understand their meaning.

Maritain's pedagogical thought is both rich and profound; it is rich from an ancient tradition that goes back to Greek thought enhanced by the contribution of medieval thinkers, especially of Saint Augustine and Saint Thomas, open to the contributions of modern thought and on the lookout for contemporary problems. His pedagogical thought is expressed in works of a relatively limited character if it is compared to the totality of his work. Maritain has not written important works in the philosophy of education comparable to *The Degrees of Knowledge* or *Creative Intuition in Art and Poetry; Education at the Crossroads* and *The Education of Man* mainly originate from lectures on pedagogy, which in no way lessens their philosophical value, but involves the disadvantage of this kind of presentation, namely the brevity with which certain questions are dealt.[4]

Nova et vetera (the new and the old): "The thought is new, but springing forth from that of Saint Thomas and even from the school of Saint Thomas. For its faithfulness to the Thomistic framework and apparatus, is derived from a strict fidelity to Saint Thomas' thought. Even when it flows from ancient sources, the thought is new because it is alive, applied to the solution of problems typical of our age, and, still more deepened and improved in accordance with its own genius."[5] Isn't that one of the basic traits of the vitality which is found in any genuine intellectual life? Change amid continuity, a real progress can only be achieved if it has its source in a living tradition. A living tradition is expressed in a gushing and renewed vitality allowing it to bear fruit in the future.

Maritain has well expressed this aspect of his thought in the following description: "A true conservative, then, is a man who is reverent towards the past, and yet is keenly aware of changing times and of the needs of the future. He will decline neither to the Left hand, nor to the Right."[6] A way of thinking both old and new which proposes nothing revolutionary (if that is understood

---

[4]   By way of example, let us point out, "the fundamental dispositions to be fostered" to which Maritain devotes only three pages (C, p. 36-38).

[5]   Presentation in *Jacques Maritain, Son oeuvre philosophique, Revue thomiste*, 1948, p. V.

[6]   "Right" and "Left" in *Blackfriars*, Oxford, Vol. XVIII, Nov., 1937, #. 212, pp. 811-812. "A static philosophy would be contrary to his Thomism, a philosophy of movement and development. Indeed, the problems of the contemporary world have profoundly influenced the

as an untimely and radical transformation of social and political structures), but recalls in season and out of season that human progress cannot be realized if it is not in and by a spiritual and internal revolution, that of the mind and the heart, making possible the conquest of personal freedom and social freedoms in an effort and joy constantly renewed, and, as a consequence, susceptible of leading to the most profound social transformations in a respect for man and his real advancement.

II.- A PEDAGOGY FOR OUR TIME

Does that mean that Maritain's educational thought could become a "fashionable" philosophy? In one sense, this would be to greatly delude oneself. Moreover, it probably shouldn't be welcomed for nothing goes out of style more quickly than fashion. We should hope that it will especially attract the attention of philosophers and educators, since it could surely contribute to an enrichment of contemporary pedagogical thought and education.

Maritain's philosophy has already known its moments of glory. It is not our intention to try and establish a summary of all that has been written about Maritain's thought,[7] nor to take inventory of the real influence that his thought may have had and still has on men; this would be an impossible evaluation to establish, at least in its second part, which is the most important.

However, perhaps it is relevant to quote the remarks of Jean Lacombe on Maritain's influence. "Jacques Maritain's destiny seems to want to thwart his influence in his own country, since it caused him to live outside of France for almost twenty years, and this long absence facilitated the lack of attention given to a magisterial work and an exemplary personality. Besides, it must be well recognized that French thought has shown itself more allergic than others to the great Aristotelian and Thomistic themes... The influence and credit which Maritain enjoys in the New World are, as is well known, of an exceptional breadth and force."[8]

The presence of Maritain's thought in America and especially in Latin America has surely been very remarkable; the testimony of Tristan d'Athaïde leaves no doubt in this regard. "From 1925 until now, I believe no European thinker has been the object in America of so many references, quotations, commentaries, books published for and against his ideas, special editions of

development of his philosophy, for he has always been concerned with the existential conditions that shape the present." B.W. SMITH, *Jacques Maritain, Antimodern or Ultramodern*, p. 51.

"Jacques Maritain has tried to be receptive to truth wherever it may be and from wherever it may come. Philosophical work discovers, invents and forges new truths within a tradition unceasingly renewed, rectified and enriched." Marie-Odile MÉTRAL, Preface to *Pour une philosophie de l'éducation*, 1969, p. 14.

[7] There is no complete bibliography of Maritain's works and of writings about him. The most important bibliography (practically complete up to 1961) is that of D. and I. GALLAGHER, *The Achievement of Jacques and Raissa Maritain. A Bibliography 1906-1961* (New York: Doubleday, 1962). An important complement to this bibliography will be found in B.W. SMITH, *Jacques Maritain, Antimodern or Ultramodern* (New York: Elsevier, 1976).

[8] Jean LACOMBE, "Jacques Maritain", in M.F. SCIACCA (ed.), *Les grands courants de la pensée mondiale contemporaine*, tome 3, *Portraits*, second volume (Milan: Marzorati, 1964), pp. 1034-1035.

newspapers and journals, and study centres in his name."[9] *Integral Humanism* has been the "bible" of the political involvement of Christians in Latin America for a number of years. This work of Maritain's has also been at the centre of a virulent polemic having as its purpose Maritain's condemnation by Rome.[10]

In the United States of America there are numerous books on the philosophy of education in which Maritain has a place alongside of great names like Plato, Aristotle, Rousseau, Kant, Dewey, etc. The literature of educational philosophy in the French language rediscovered "the forgotten figure" whose name appears in Jacques Ulmann's *La pensée éducative contemporaine*.[11] People began then to take an interest in the work of a man who has presented almost all his pedagogical reflections before American audiences, and it is only fitting that Maritain should have his place in the great debates on education when the school is questioned and educational thought seems marked by uncertainty.

For the educational thought of Maritain is remarkably up to date; Maritain is a pedagogue of our time and for our time. (We would need to write another book on this topic.)

There can be no question of presenting here a picture of the totality of the crucial problems of contemporary education.[12] Several national and international commissions have concentrated attentively on the "dead ends" of our educational systems.

There is no miraculous solution to these problems, but the proposed remedies show some convergence, especially the slanting of education in the direction of total and lifelong education, the establishment of a pedagogy centred on the learner and directed toward autodidacticism, the increased importance of general culture as a means of fostering a balanced human development, the ability to adapt oneself to change, the capacity to intelligently assume democratic responsibilities.

Beneath these different converging elements and others, who does not see that, ultimately, today's education and that of tomorrow must busy itself with what is essential, that is, with the human person. "The function of an education which is adapted to current needs is, surely, as it has always been, concerned with 'learning to be', to use a recent and already celebrated phrase or, as a poet has said, 'learning the job of living, a hard and worthy trade'."[13]

---

[9] Tristan D'ATHAIDE (Alceu Amoroso Lima), "Maritain et l'Amérique latine", in *Revue thomiste*, Special Issue devoted to Jacques Maritain, Vol. 48, 1948 # 1 and 2, p. 16.

[10] This was a bad business, and unsuccessful, in which the theologian Garrigou — Lagrange became involved in spite of himself. See Julio MEINVIELLE, *Correspondance avec le R.P. Garrigou-Lagrange à propos de Lammenais et Maritain*, 1947; and Jacques MARITAIN, *Raison et Raisons*, pp. 271-285.

[11] Jacques ULMANN. *La pensée éducative contemporaine* (Paris: PUF, 1976), pp. 46-47.

[12] Some recent works deal with these problems, particularly, Edgar FAURE et alii, *Learning to Be* (Paris: Unesco; London: Harrap, 1972); Jean THOMAS, *World Problems in Education: A Brief Analytical Survey* (Paris: Unesco, 1975); Guy AVANZINI et alii, *La pédagogie au 20ᵉ siècle* (Toulouse: Privat, 1975).

[13] Jean THOMAS. *World Problems in Education: A Brief Analytical Survey*, p. 32.

But yet do we know what it is to be a man? It is indeed at this level that the crisis of civilization, our crisis, shows itself, the crisis of civilization which has profound repercussions on the family, the society but also on the schools and universities which are much more the victims than the cause of the many difficulties assailing them.

Maritain is well aware of this profound crisis, with a consciousness expressing itself with a certain disillusionment, but with the hope as well "that after a particularly formidable historical ordeal, Western civilization will regenerate itself" (PE, 114).

Our civilization is in a state of crisis and this crisis is situated in the depths of the human being; it concerns neither more nor less than a "spiritual rout", characterized by the absence of a philosophy of life which would allow men to understand the reasons they have to live and die, Victor Frankl's "meaninglessness".

It would seem that technocracy "that is to say technology understood and revered in such a way as to exclude any higher wisdom and any endeavour to understand something other than calculable phenomena" (PE, 116), has become the new wisdom of our society. Megalopolis and the organization man progressively creep into daily life and attempt to take the place of the values of the person, and his freedom, of truth, love and God. Under technocracy, human life becomes more and more fragmented, "functionalized" (fewer and fewer persons and more "functionaries" are encountered); human life is subject to more and more complicated administrative structures which exercise a new form of totalitarianism (the great academic institutions are not exempt from it) whose counterpart seems to be the leveling of values, a materialism leaving to men only the challenge of becoming consumers who are never satisfied, fostering "progress" according to the demands of an economic system whose ideal is a progressive and endless increase of the *gross national product*. "The entirely materialist residue of social formation that is called the consumer society appears, despite so many partial advances which follow their course, as the trade-mark and standard of a civilization in complete disintegration" (PE, 114).

This sketch all too short of contemporary society in a state of crisis drawn by Maritain, however much of a caricature it may be, reveals an important truth charged with consequences for the educational systems which reflect, at least in part, the social environment in which they are inserted and its culture.

It can be legitimately said that the crisis in education is a reflection of the contemporary crisis of civilization. Striking events like those of May, 1968 in France make us more acutely aware of this crisis even if they do so in a brutal way. The students who took part in these events — and in similar occurrences in a number of countries — were not all revolutionaries "trained in the best tactical and psychological procedures in rival vanguard groups, with anarchical tendencies or unorthodox Marxists, to which they belong, and knowing full well what they wanted: upsetting not only the university, but the entire social life of the country, by enlisting the student revolt under the banner of the alleged fecundity of pure chaos" (PE, 118).

However, for a large number of students, it was a process of becoming aware "of a vast human disorder, social and political as well as intellectual". Of course, they blamed "the poor organization of studies, the absence of practical employment"; but, more profoundly "it is *metaphysical evil* which, even if one was not prepared to become aware of it, made itself felt in the very depths of the mind, and which affects the youth more cruelly because they are not yet hardened to self-deception. I mean the emptiness, the complete annihilation of any absolute value and of any faith in the truth to which youth is consigned by the dominant intellectual elite and by a secondary and university education which by and large (and in spite of many individual exceptions) lightly betrays its essential mission. Contemporary youth have been systematically deprived *of any reason for living"* (PE, 119).

As a consequence of University protest movements, university education has been re-examined, palpable progress toward multi-disciplinary studies and student participation has been achieved. Time has been spent on the structural elements of university reform and, for many, that was already too much of a concession to make to small overly noisy groups of students. It is said that the proof of it has already been shown, for, after several enthusiastic years facing the new situation, students and even professors seem already winded by a structural participation which requires a lot of energy and seems somewhat fruitless.

Have the depths of the problem really been plumbed? Have educators examined sufficiently the fundamental demands of youth and, as a consequence, re-examined the aims of education?

What is this youth that Maritain views with love, anguish and trust? "I like and respect contemporary youth, and I contemplate them with a strange feeling of anguish. They know a great deal about matter, natural facts, and human facts, but almost nothing about the soul" (C, 86).[14]

This youth has undergone an important cultural change; they live existentially according to characteristics calling to mind the natural goodness of which Rousseau dreamed. "For they are good indeed and generous and free, and they even display, in noble as well as in immoral deeds, a kind of

---

[14] "to live in a state of doubt as regards not phenomena, but the ultimate realities the knowledge of which is a natural possibility, privilege, and duty for human intelligence, is to live more miserably than animals, which at least tend with instinctive and buoyant certitude toward the ends of their ephemeral life" (C, 116-117).

"Five years of medecine and a credit of fifteen hours in ethics... on the enormous issues which arise daily in a doctor's office, and on an art of living that contemporary society and contemporary man seek through health, education or work." Jacques GRAND'MAISON. *Pour une pédagogie sociale d'autodéveloppement en éducation* (Montreal: Stanké, 1976), p. 33.

"Too many indicators point out to us the current need to rediscover an internal structure, a coherent and deeper personal reflection, not to welcome an education more mindful of this" (*ibid.*, p. 67).

Jacques Grand'Maison, in this very fine book on education, expresses pedagogical concerns and a philosophy of education akin to the educational thought of Maritain.

purity which resembles the innocence of birds and deer... They stand in goodness upon nothing" (C, 86).[15]

The crisis of civilization that we know, they live concretely and often in a dramatic way, and they express it with a simplicity and frankness of which adults seem incapable.

Our society, invaded by technology and the growing complexity of the socialization process, leaves less and less living space for the expression of freedom and inter-personal relationships. Anonymity is the human environment, pragmatism its climate and consumption its objective.

Young people are trained in the sciences and techniques, but they are "miserably ignorant of everything that concerns God and the deepest realities in man and the world. What we are faced with, in this regard, is a kind of regular frustration — by adults and the general organization of teaching — of certain of the most vital needs and aspirations, and even of the basic rights of intellectual nature of young persons" (EM, 55).

Beneath their occasionally inopportune spontaneity a deep suffering and profound uneasiness is hidden: "Anxiety and thirst arise in a number of them, and this very fact is a reason for hope" (C, 87).

It could be that one of the most urgent tasks of educators is to help youth rediscover faith in human reason, the natural faith of reason in the truth which sets us free, to help them give themselves the "addition of soul" which the world urgently needs.

It could also be that in the midst of the "conflicts and uncertainties" of contemporary pedagogy, Maritain's pedagogical thought can stimulate minds in this direction and bring a substantial contribution to the necessary rediscovery of the values of the person, and of truth and freedom.[16]

III.- A SOURCE FOR EXPLORATION

If it is the case that contemporary man and his education suffer from *metaphysical evil*, that is, from the absence of reasons for living and uncertainty about the meaning of human existence, ultimately from the lack of

---

[15] One should add that perhaps for the first time our society experiences the existence of an important stratum of the population which is called the youth.

Maritain's evocation of the traits of contemporary youth shows some similarity to some recent and easily available studies: See, for instance, Charles A. REICH. *The Greening of America* (New York: A Bantam Book, 1971), and J.-F. SIX, *Les jeunes, l'avenir et la foi* (Paris: Desclée de Brouwer, 1976).

When he thinks of the education of youth, Maritain includes in his perspectives and concerns both young men and women (see, for example, C, 75); he has not suggested a particular kind of education for either one of these groups.

The only explicit text, in this regard, is an excerpt from a speech given in 1941 and published under the title "The Education of Women (in EM, 154-158); in this passage, he places in evidence the specific intellectual qualities of women.

[16] "In fact education has most often lost its philosophical roots. It is for philosophical reasons, relying on a philosophically based humanism, that Jacques Maritain offers sometimes impertinent reflections because they are pertinent for a human and fully democratic education." Marie-Odile Métral, Preface to *Pour une philosophie de l'éducation*, 1969, pages 11-12.

faith in the human person, in his intellect and freedom, it might very well be that Maritain's thought is a source to explore[17] deserving our attention.

Maritain's pedagogical work, in spite of its obvious limitations, conceals a treasure on which it is worthwhile concentrating. That is what we have tried to do in the present work which attempts to reflect the deep intentions of his thought, to place in evidence, under the heading of the *education for freedom*, the basic articulations of his pedagogical thought in their continuity with their philosophical foundations.

By way of a brief summary, let us recall the major themes of his pedagogical thought: the metaphysics of the person as a being of knowledge and love; the person as a whole and also as a part of society; freedom as expression and progressive movement of the person; the aims of education and its dynamics as human awakening and as progressive conquest of freedom through truth, wisdom and love (love of the Good, of others and of God); the rediscovery of liberal education for all in secondary education and its expression in a new arrangement of the humanities; the sense of universality tied to advanced university specialization: moral education, scholastic pluralism and the Christian school.

Maritain could certainly make an important contribution to the many dialogues, the great debates currently on education, for instance the debates relating to the "liberterian" approach versus the "progressive" approach, the debates about academic reforms at the secondary school as well as at the university, etc., with a view to rediscovering the meaning of man, his education and his freedom.

On the other hand, in order to better serve the human person, Maritain's thought would have to be made more explicit on a number of points; it would be enriched through contact with the sciences of education[18], and from being the object of a study comparing it with other philosophies of education; these are so many tasks that the "disciples" of Maritain should undertake if they want his pedagogical thought to be more fruitful.

It is to Maritain's credit to offer a pedagogical thought for contemporary reflection in which "the direction of the process and hierarchy of values

---

[17]   "If Mr. Snyders is completely right to stress the idea of truth and to show that, without reference to it, there is no serious education, then today we cannot hope to reach agreement on his proposition. In his very fine work *Pour une philosophie de l'éducation*, Jacques Maritain recommends the inclusion of theology as an option in the educational programs at the second degree. If all do not share Maritain's faith, they will acknowledge with him — and with Mr. Snyders — that faith is indispensable for the emergence and rise of a truly educational dynamics; but precisely, its absence and, more generally, the loss of aims are the major reason for the contemporary crisis of the School as well as the totality of formative influences which seemingly know less and less where they are heading." Guy AVANZINI, "Des finalités introuvables", in *La pédagogie au 20ᵉ siècle* (Toulouse: Privat, 1975), p. 365.

[18]   We believe in a possibly fruitful collaboration between the philosophy of education and the sciences of education.

"Far from being opposed or in competition both are required together; their twofold ascent cannot be dissociated and their relation functions by way of mutual stimulation." Guy AVANZINI. *Introduction aux sciences de l'éducation* (Toulouse: Privat, 1976), p. 113.

which it implies" are clearly expounded and rationally justified; this is no mean thing in our uncertain world. Maritain offers his thoughts for the reflection of those of us who are the "Pilgrims of the Absolute"[19]; he expounds them with openness of mind and frankness.

> Education provides the great peaceful means of improving society; and yet, as we have seen, the character of education is determined by the character of society. Still we must not assume a defeatist attitude. The alternative to a spiritual revolution is a political revolution. I rather prefer the former. The only way to secure a spiritual revolution is through Education.[20]

The spiritual revolution spoken of by Hutchins is indeed the one to which Maritain invites us through *an education for freedom;* true liberation and revolution have their roots in the inwardness of the human person and require an education whose primary end is "liberation through knowledge and wisdom, good will, and love" (C, 11).

No revolution can replace the spiritual revolution, none is more worthy of man. It is the most difficult to realize, it is also the most uplifting for the human person whose vocation is for freedom.

---

[19]   Léon Bloy, the friend and godparent of Jacques and Raissa Maritain called himself gladly the "Pilgrim of the Absolute". See Raïssa MARITAIN, *We Have Been Friends Together and Adventures in Grace* (New York: Doubleday, 1961), pp. 95 and 140.

[20]   Robert M. HUTCHINS, *Education for Freedom* (Baton Rouge, Louisiana: State University Press, 1943), pp. 58-59.

Bibliography

We confine our bibliography to Maritain's works and to other writings of which explicit mention has been made or which have been quoted.

It consists of four parts: 1) Maritain's works on freedom and on education. (We thought it was useful to annotate the works listed in this first part.) 2. Other works of Maritain referred to in the present work. 3. Writings about Maritain. 4. Other writings.

1. MARITAIN'S WORKS ON FREEDOM AND EDUCATION

FREEDOM

Freedom in the Modern World (New York: Charles Scribner's Sons, 1936), 223 pages. Trans. Richard O'SULLIVAN

> The first part of the book (pp. 3-73) is devoted to "a philosophy of freedom which Maritain sets out in three steps:
> — Freedom presupposes nature and is rooted in reason.
> — Freedom is distinct from nature and constitutes a separate and inviolable world.
> — Our freedom of spontaneity develops starting with an initial freedom up to the terminal freedom which is freedom of autonomy. This conquest of freedom can and must be achieved on the spiritual as on the social plane.

"The Conquest of Freedom," in Ruth Nanda ANSHEN (ed.), *Freedom, Its Meaning* (London: George Allen and Unwin, 1942), 335 pages. Trans. Harry MCNEILL and Emmanuel CHAPMAN

> Maritain deals with the conquest of freedom in the first chapter of *Principes d'une politique humaniste,* translated here (pp. 210-228). Freedom of autonomy presupposes the freedom of choice through which we can conquer our perfection and our autonomy, that is, respond to the aspirations of the person as human (through political emancipation) and in so far as a person (the conquest of spiritual freedom).

The Range of Reason (New York: Charles Scribner's Sons, 1952), 226 pages.

> In Chapter VI, Maritain explains how a child, in the first truly free and good act, deliberates on the meaning of his life and chooses the *Bonum honestum,* thus implicitly ordering himself in a lived act to God (without being aware of it). Following that he gives an account of the influence of grace in regard to this free act.

Scholasticism and Politics (New York: Doubleday and Company, 1960), 233 pages. Trans. edited by Mortimer J. ADLER

> Chapter V (pp. 117-138) contains a statement of the Thomist idea of freedom. After having distinguished the freedom of spontaneity from the freedom of choice, Maritain shows how freedom of choice is possible by reason of the very nature of the will as intellectual appetite, and how it needs the mutual causality of the intellect and the will for its exercise; then he outlines the conquest of freedom in the order of social life in its most general features.

De Bergson à Thomas d'Aquin. Essais de métaphysique et de morale (Paris: Paul Hartmann, 1947), 333 pages.

> Chapter VI bears on the degrees of freedom of spontaneity and on the spontaneity appropriate to the human person (which is independence) to conquer on the personal level as on the social (pp. 221-249).

Bergsonian Philosophy and Thomism (New York: Philosophical Library, 1955), 383 pages Translated by M.I. and J.G. ANDISON.

Maritain devotes the sixth chapter of this book (pp. 252-277), to the problem of freedom. After having stated the Bergsonian solution which seems anti-intellectualist to him, Maritain shows how "the whole root of freedom is constituted in the intellect" according to the scholastic philosophy of freedom.

EDUCATION

Preface to Frans DE HOVRE, *Essai de la philosophie pédagogique,* translated from Flemish by G. SIMEONS (Brussels: Albert DeWit, 1927), pages VII-XI.

In this preface which is his first text on education, Maritain explains how pedagogy is based on a conception of life and results from philosophy, and that, to the extent to which the end of human life is supernatural, educational science is linked with theology. He concludes by suggesting that Thomistic thought could bring a valuable contribution to the educational theory of our time.

Education at the Crossroads (New Haven: Yale University Press, 1943), 120 pages. Based on the Terry Lectures delivered at Yale University.

These four lectures are in reality a short treatise on the philosophy of education. In them, Maritain presents the essentials of his educational thought in four chapters, under the following titles:

1. *The Aims of Education:* education presupposes a philosophy of man. Because man is a person and free, the aims of education are primarily the conquest of internal freedom, and, in the second place, the meaning of social freedom and social responsibility.

2. *The Dynamics of Education:* Maritain explains the instrumental role of the teacher whose authority is "the duty of the adult towards the child". In order to carry out well his role of human wakener, the teacher should foster in the child the feeling for the truth, for the good and for justice, an openness in regard to existence, the sense of a job well done and the spirit of cooperation. He should encourage the child by being mindful of his inner resources, by nourishing his inner unity and by freeing his intellect through the mastery of reason over the things learned.

3. *The Humanities and Liberal Education.* After having shown that the three great stages of education are based on the three natural periods in the development of the intellect, Maritain explains his conception of liberal education for all and the program of secondary education which flows from it. Then he closes the chapter by defining the curriculum of the ideal university as centre of specialized education animated by the spirit of universality.

4. *The Trials of Present-Day* Education. In the post-war world, the urgency of an integral education for an integral humanism is evident, as well as is the need for a liberal education faithful to its essential goals, to which is added an additional burden especially in the realm of moral teaching.

L'éducation à la croisée des chemins. Preface by Charles JOURNET (Paris: Egloff, 1947), 239 pages.

The book is the French version of *Education at the Crossroads.* In addition to Charles Journet's preface, Maritain adds to it, in an appendix, a very thought-provoking text on "the problem of the public school in France" examined in the light of pluralism.

"Moral Education", in *A College goes to School: Centennial Lectures* (Notre Dame and Holy Cross, Indiana: St. Mary's College; and Paterson, New Jersey: St. Anthony Guild Press, 1945), pp. 1-25.

In this lecture, Maritain deals successively with the role of the school in regard to moral education, the concrete bonds which exist between ethics and religion, the basic role of the family in moral education and with moral teaching in the school.

"Thomist Views on Education", in *Modern Philosophies and Education,* edited by Nelson B. HENRY (Chicago: University of Chicago Press, 1955), pp. 57-90.

This article like *Education at the Crossroads* is a statement of Maritain's views on education. However, it differs in style. Here we find a synthesis, sometimes quite compact, of his basic positions on man and knowledge, on the goals and values of education, on the educational process, on the school and society, on the school and religion. In regard to each question, Maritain first articulates philosophical principles in order subsequently to consider their practical application in education.

"On Some Typical Aspects of Christian Education", in Edmond FULLER (ed.), *The Christian Idea of Education* (New Haven: Yale University Press, 1957), pp. 173-198 (address given at a Seminar on Christian Education at the Kent School, November, 1955).

    In this lecture, Maritain defines the Christian idea of man and its implications for Christian education. In addition to the needs of any genuine education, Christian education has its specific requirements, especially the inclusion of the great Christian classics in the humanities; the formation of the Christian intellect through philosophy, theology and Sacred Scripture; the strengthening of spiritual life through liturgical groups and groups studying the Bible and the great spiritual writers.

"Moral and Spiritual Values in Education", Proceedings of the Eighty Ninth Convocation of the Board of Regents of the University of the State of New York, April 25, 1958, pp. 14-21.

    This brief statement takes up once more, in summary fashion, Maritain's main ideas on moral education and the role of the school in regard to it.

Pour une philosophie de l'éducation (Paris: Fayard, Les Idées et la vie, 1959), 249 pages.

    This book reunites in a single volume Maritain's principal writings on education. The first part is a reproduction of *Education at the Crossroads*. The second part includes the French version of "Thomist View on Education" and "On Some Typical Aspects of Christian Education". The text on "the problem of the public school in France" is reproduced in an appendix.

Pour une philosophie de l'éducation, nouvelle édition revue et complétée (Paris: Fayard, 1969), 198 pages.

    This is a new revised and completed edition of the 1959 publication. Several minor changes may be noted in the text and two more important changes: the first relates to the conception of the university which should leave practical subjects to professional schools (while Maritain had suggested in the first edition the reorganization of all subjects in the university); the second change consists in some new considerations on the demands of the present day and of the future and on the Events of May, 1968 in France (chapter 4). Marie-Odile Métral's preface is added to this edition.

The Education of Man: The Educational Philosophy of Jacques Maritain. Edited and with an Introduction by Donald and Idella GALLAGHER (Notre Dame: University of Notre Dame Press, 1963), 191 pages.

    This book published through the diligence of Donald and Idella Gallagher (who have written a very fine introduction to it) is intended to be the English complement of *Education at the Crossroads* and includes Maritain's principal texts on education.

2. OTHER WORKS OF MARITAIN REFERRED TO IN THE PRESENT WORK

A Preface to Metaphysics: Seven Lectures on Being (New York and London: Sheed and Ward, 1939), 152 pages.

"About Christian Philosophy", in *The Human Person and the World of Values, A Tribute to Dietrich Von Hildebrand by his friends in Philosophy,* Edited by Barduin V. SCHWARZ (New York: Fordham University Press, 1960), pp. 1-10.

An Essay on Christian Philosophy. Trans. Edward H. FLANNERY (New York: Philosophical Library, 1955), 116 pages.

An Introduction to Philosophy. Trans. E.I. WATKIN (London and New York: Sheed and Ward, 1930), 207 pages.

Antimoderne, New and enlarged edition (Paris: Editions de la Revue des Jeunes et Desclée et Cie., 1922), 266 pages.

Approches sans entraves, a work published by le Cercle d'études Jacques et Raïssa Maritain. Preface by Ernst R. KORN (Paris: Fayard, 1973), 595 pages.

Art and Faith: Letters Between Jacques Maritain and Jean Cocteau. Trans. John COLEMAN (New York: Philosophical Library, 1948), 138 pages.

Carnet de notes (Paris: Desclée de Brouwer, 1965), 415 pages.

Christianity and Democracy. Trans. Doris C. ANSON (New York: Charles Scribner's Sons, 1944), 98 pages.

"Confession of Faith," *The Social and Political Philosophy of Jacques Maritain.* Edited by Joseph W. EVANS and Leo R. WARD (New York: Charles Scribner's Sons, 1955), pp. 331-343.

Creative Intuition in Art and Poetry (New York: Pantheon Books, 1953), 339 pages.

Distinguish to Unite, or The Degrees of Knowledge. Trans under the supervision of Gerald B. PHELAN (New York: Charles Scribner's Sons, 1959; London: G. Bles, 1959), 476 pages.

Dream of Descartes. Trans. Mabelle L. ANDISON (New York: Philosophical Library, 1944), 220 pages.

Existence and the Existent. Trans. Lewis GALANTIÈRE and Gerald B. PHELAN (New York: Pantheon Books, 1948), 148 pages.

God and the Permission of Evil. Trans. Joseph W. EVANS (Milwaukee: The Bruce Publishing Company, 1966), 121 pages.

"Il n'y a pas de savoir sans intuitivité," in *Revue thomiste,* 1970, pp. 30-71.

Integral Humanism: Temporal and Spiritual Problems of a New Christendom. Trans. Joseph W. EVANS (New York: Charles Scribner's Sons, 1968), 308 pages.

Le philosophe dans la cité (Paris: Alsatia, 1960), 205 pages.

La signification de l'athéisme contemporain (Paris: Desclée de Brouwer, 1949), 42 pages.

"Le thomisme et la civilisation," *Revue de philosophie,* Vol. XXXV, 1928, pp. 109-140.

Man and the State (Chicago: University of Chicago Press, 1951), 219 pages.

Moral Philosophy — An Historical and Critical Survey of the Great Systems (New York: Charles Scribner's Sons, 1964), 468 pages.

On the Use of Philosophy (Princeton: Princeton University Press, 1961), 71 pages.

On the Philosophy of History. Edited by Joseph W. EVANS (New York: Charles Scribner's Sons, 1957), 180 pages.

Preface in Henry BARS, *La politique selon Jacques Maritain* (Paris: Les Editions ouvrières, 1961), pp. 7-14.

Quatre essais sur l'esprit dans sa condition charnelle. New revised and enlarged edition (Paris: Alsatia, 1956), 272 pages.

Questions de conscience. Essais et allocutions. (Paris: Desclée de Brouwer, 1938), 279 pages.

Réflexions sur l'intelligence et sur sa vie propre (Paris: Nouvelle Librairie nationale, Bibliothèque française de philosophie, 1924), 378 pages.

"Réflexions sur la nature blessée et sur l'intuition de l'être," *Revue thomiste,* Vol. LXVIII, 1968), pp. 5-40.

Religion and Culture. Trans. J.F. SCANLAN (London: Sheed and Ward, 1931), 66 pages.

"Right" and "Left", *Blackfriars* (Oxford: Blackfriars), Vol. XVIII, Nov., 1937, No. 212, pp. 807-812. *Blackfriars* is a montly review edited by English Dominicans.

Saint Thomas Aquinas. Trans. Joseph W. EVANS and Peter O'REILLY (New York: Meridian Books, 1958), 281 pages.

Science and Wisdom. Trans. Bernard WALL (New York: Charles Scribner's Sons, 1940; London: G. Bles, 1940), 241 pages.

"Socrate et la philosophie morale," *Mélanges offerts à Etienne Gilson* (Paris: Vrin, 1959), pp. 389-402.

Sort de l'homme (Neuchâtel: Editions de la Baconnière, 1943), 155 pages.

"Sur l'éthique bergsonienne", *Revue de métaphysique et de morale,* 1959, pp. 141-160.

The Peasant of the Garonne: An Old Layman Questions Himself about the Present Time. Trans. Michael CUDDIHY and Elizabeth HUGHES (New York: Holt, Rinehart and Winston, 1968), 277 pages.

The Person and the Common Good. Trans. John J. FITZGERALD (Notre Dame: University of Notre Dame Press, 1966), 108 pages.

The Rights of Man and Natural Law. Trans. Doris C. ANSON (New York: Charles Scribner's Sons, 1943), 63 pages.

Theonas: Conversations of a Sage. Trans. F.J. SHEED (New York: Sheed and Ward, 1935), 200 pages.

Three Reformers: Luther, Descartes, Rousseau (London: Sheed and Ward, 1935), 234 pages.

3. WRITINGS ON MARITAIN

BARS, Henry, *Maritain en notre temps* (Paris: Grasset, 1959), 397 pages.

BARS, Henry, *Sujet et subjectivité selon Jacques Maritain, in Les Etudes philosophiques,* Special Issue Devoted to Gabriel Marcel, Jacques Maritain, Jean Wahl, (Paris: P.U.F. janvier-mars 1975), pp. 31-46.

BRUNNER, Fernand, *Allocation d'ouverture, in Actes du XVIᵉ Congrès des Sociétés de philosophie de langue française* (Reims, 3-6 septembre 1974), *La Culture,* Vander-Nauwelaerts, 1975.

CROTEAU, Jacques, o.m.i., *Les fondements thomistes du personnalisme de Maritain* (Ottawa: Les Editions de l'Université d'Ottawa, 1955), 267 pages.

DE FINANCE, Joseph, s.j., *La philosophie de la liberté chez Maritain, in Recherches et débats,* n° 19 (Paris: Fayard, 1957), pp. 95-116.

EVANS, Joseph W., "Jacques Maritain", *The New Scholasticism,* Maritains' Ninetieth Birthday, Vol. XLVI, 1972, pp. 2-9.

FECHER, Charles A., *The Philosophy of Jacques Maritain* (Westminster (Maryland): The Newman Press, 1953), XIV-361 pages.

GALLAGHER, Donald & Idella, *Introduction. Toward a Christian Philosophy of Education,* in Jacques MARITAIN, *The Education of Man* (Notre-Dame: University of Notre-Dame Press, 1963), pp. 9-31.

GALLAGHER, Donald & Idella, *The Achievement of Jacques and Raïssa Maritain, A bibliography 1906-1961* (New York: Doubleday and Company, Inc. 1962), 256 pages.

Jacques Maritain, in *Recherches et débats*, 19 (Paris: Fayard, 1957), 218 pages.

Jacques Maritain. Son oeuvre philosophique, Bibliothèque de la Revue thomiste, Desclée de Brouwer, 1948, X11-342 pages.

Jacques Maritain. The Man and His achievement, Edited with an Introduction by Joseph W. EVANS (New York: Sheed and Ward, 1963), X11-258 pages.

JOURNET, Charles, *Foreword* to the French Edition of *Education at the Crossroads*, in Jacques MARITAIN, *Pour une philosophie de l'éducation* (Paris: Fayard, 1959), pp. 13-15.

LABOURDETTE, M.-Michel, o.p., "Connaissance pratique et savoir moral", in *Jacques Maritain. Son oeuvre philosophique, Revue thomiste*, (1948), pp. 142-179.

LACOMBE, Olivier, "Jacques Maritain et la philosophie de l'être, in *Les Etudes philosophiques*, Special Issue Devoted to Gabriel Marcel, Jacques Maritain, Jean Wahl (Paris: P.U.F., janvier-mars 1975), pp. 69-78.

LACOMBE, Jean, *Jacques Maritain*, in M.J. SCIACCA, éditeur, *Les grands courants de la pensée mondiale contemporaine*, tome 3, *Portraits*, second volume (Milan: Marzorati, 1964), pp. 1033-1052.

MARITAIN, Raïssa, *We have Been Friends Together* and *Adventures in Grace*. Trans. Julie KERNAN (New York: Doubleday and Company, Image Books, 1961), 392 pages.

MEINVIELLE, Jules, *Correspondance avec le R.P. Garrigou-Lagrange à propos de Lamenais et Maritain* (Translated from Spanish), (Buenos Aires: Editions "Nuestro Tiempo", 1947), 138 pages.

ROSSNER, William L., *"Love in the Thought of Jacques Maritain"*, *Jacques Maritain, The Man and his Achievement* (New York: Sheed and Ward, 1963), pp. 237-256.

SADLIER, M., *A Note on the Personalism of Jacques Maritain*, in *Philosophical Studies*, I, June 1951, p. 35-39 (St. Patrick's College, Maynooth, Ireland).

SMITH, Williams Brooke, *Jacques Maritain, Antimodern or Ultramodern, An Historical Analysis of His Critics, His Thought and His Life* (N.Y.: Elsevier, 1976), 194 pages.

WARD, Leo R., c.s.c., *"Maritain's Philosophy of Education"*, *Jacques Maritain. The Man and His Achievement* (N.Y.: Sheed and Ward, 1963), pp. 193-214.

4. OTHER WRITINGS

ALAIN, *Propos sur l'éducation* (Paris: P.U.F. [15ᵉ édition], 1972), 227 pages.

ALAIN, Spinoza (Paris: Gallimard [Idées], 1949), 183 pages.

AVANZINI, Guy, *Introduction aux sciences de l'éducation. Les orientations de la recherche et le développement des méthodes dans le champ de l'éducation moderne* (Toulouse: Edouard Privat ["Mésopé" Bibliothèque de l'Action sociale], 1976), 200 pages.

AVANZINI, Guy, et alii, *La pédagogie au 20ᵉ siècle* (Toulouse: Privat, 1975), 399 pages.

BONNEAU, Louis-Philippe, & CORRY, J.A., *Quest for the Optimum. Research Policies in the Universities of Canada* (Ottawa: Association of Universities and Colleges of Canada, Vol. I, 1972), v-207 pages.

The Documents of Vatican Two (New York: The America Press, 1966), pp. 637-651.

D'ATHAÏDE, Tristan (Alceu Amoroso LIMA), "Maritain et l'Amérique latine", *Revue thomiste*, Special edition devoted to Jacques Maritain, (1948), pp. 12-17.

FAURE, Edgar, et alii, *Learning to Be* (Paris: Unesco; London: Harrap, 1972), XXXIX-313 pages.

FREIRE, Paulo, *Education for Critical Consciousness* (New York: Seabury Press, 1973), 164 pages.

FREIRE, Paulo, *Pedagogy of the Oppressed* (New York: Seabury Press, 1970), 186 pages.

GRAND'MAISON, Jacques, *Pour une pédagogie sociale d'antodéveloppement en éducation* (Montréal: Editions internationales Alain Stanké Ltée, 1976), 191 pages.

HAMELINE, Daniel, & DARDELIN, Joëlle, *La liberté d'apprendre. Situation II*, (Paris: Les Editions ouvrières, 1977), 349 pages.

HUME, David, *Treatise of Human Nature* (New York: Dutton [Everyman's Library], vol. 1, 1956), XXXI-258 pages.

HUTCHINS, Robert M., *Education for Freedom*, Baton Rouge (Louisiana: Louisiana State University Press, 1943), IX-108 pages.

HUTCHINS, Robert M., *The Learning Society* (London: Pall Mall Press, 1968), XI-142 pages.

HUXLEY, Aldous, *Brave New World Revisited* (London: Chatto and Windus, 1959), 164 pages, Chapter XI, *Education for Freedom*, pp. 135-149.

HUXLEY, Aldous, *Brave New World* (Harmondsworth, England: Penguin Books, 1968), 200 pages.

LAPIERRE, Jean-William, *Un terrain de lutte*, in *La Formation permanente, Idée neuve? Idée fausse?* Special issue of the review *Esprit* (octobre 1974), pp. 457-469.

MARCEL, Gabriel, "La liberté en 1971", in *Les Etudes philosophiques* (Paris: P.U.F., janvier-mars 1975), pp. 7-17.

MOUROUX, Jean, *The Meaning of Man* (London: Sheed and Ward, 1948), 304 pages.

NEILL, A.S., *Summerhill* (Harmondsworth; Penguin, 1971) 336 pages.

PARAIN-VIAL, Jeanne, *La liberté et les sciences de l'homme* (Toulouse: "Nouvelle Recherche", Privat, 1973), 169 pages.

PASCAL, Georges, *Alain éducateur*, 2ᵉ édition (Paris: P.U.F., 1969), 122 pages.

REBOUL, Olivier, *La philosophie de l'éducation*, 2ᵉ édition revue et augmentée, (Paris: P.U.F. [Le philosophe], 1976), 134 pages.

REBOUL, Olivier, *L'endoctrinement* (Paris: P.U.F. [L'éducateur], 1977), 197 pages.

ROUSSEAU, Jean-Jacques, *Emile* (New York: E.P. Dutton, 1930), 444 pages.

SARTRE, Jean-Paul, *Existentialism and Humanism* (London: Methuen, 1960), 70 pages.

SNYDERS, Georges, *Où vont les pédagogies non-directives?* 3ᵉ édition (Paris: P.U.F., 1975), 378 pages.

THOMAS, Jean, *World Problems in Education* (Paris: Unesco Press, 1975), 166 pages.

ULMANN, Jacques, *La nature et l'éducation. L'idée de nature dans l'éducation physique et dans l'éducation morale* (Paris: Librairie philosophique Vrin [Bibliothèque d'histoire de la philosophie], 1974), 599 pages.

ULMANN, Jacques, *La pensée éducative contemporaine* (Paris: P.U.F., 1976), 157 pages.

VERNEAUX, Roger, *Philosophie de l'homme*, Nouvelle édition (Paris: Beauchesne [Cours de philosophie thomiste], 1956), 190 pages.

VIOLA, Francesco, "La liberté humaine entre liberté absolue et déterminisme", dans *Nova et Vetera*, L1ᵉ année, n° 2 (avril-juin 1976), p. 116-131.

WHITEHEAD, Alfred North, *The Aims of Education, and Other Essays*, 13th printing (The New American Library, A Mentor Book, 1963), XI-158 pages.

Achevé d'imprimer
en juin mil neuf cent quatre-vingt-deux
sur les presses de l'Imprimerie Gagné Ltée
Louiseville - Montréal.
Imprimé au Canada

FRANKLIN AND MARSHALL COLLEGE
LB880.M3332 A4413   010101 000
Allard, Jean Louis.
Education for freedom : the ph

0 1114 0139141 7

LB
880
.M3332-
A4413

DEC 3 1984	DATE DUE	
5-24-98FLL		